Daily Express

ALL
COLOUR
COOKERY
BOOK

Daily Express

ALL COLOUR COOKERY BOOK

WILLI ELSENER

SUNBURST BOOKS

AUTHOR'S ACKNOWLEDGEMENTS

My most sincere thanks to:

The Dorchester Management
for their constant support of my original column for The Daily Express

Louis Stanley
for introducing me to The Daily Express

Jayne Elsener, my wife
for her unfailing encouragement and assistance

Sylvia Baumann
for typing and testing the recipes

Robert Gleeson, Stuart Pate and Jamie Walker
for testing the recipes

Rebecca Meagher
for her photography

Thomas Goode & Co.
for the use of their china

Sara Colledge
for editing the recipes and text

and
to all those who have kindly assisted me.

Without the above people, it would not have been possible to produce this book.

This edition first published 1994 by Sunburst Books,
Deacon House, 65 Old Church Street, London SW3 5BS.

ISBN 1 85778 099 X
Printed and bound in Hong Kong

CONTENTS

DESSERTS AND CAKES

MISCELLANEOUS

CONVERSION TABLES

All these are approximate conversions, which have been rounded up or down. In a few recipes it has been necessary to modify them, so please always follow the amounts listed in each recipe. Also, never mix metric and imperial in the same recipe - this may affect the final result.

OVEN TEMPERATURES

GAS MARK	°F	°C
1	275	140
2	300	150
3	325	170
4	350	180
5	375	190
6	400	200
7	425	220
8	450	230
9	475	240

WEIGHT

METRIC	IMPERIAL
15 g	½ oz
25 g	1 oz
50 g	2 oz
75 g	3 oz
100-125 g	4 oz
150 g	5 oz
175 g	6 oz
200 g	7 oz
225 g	8 oz (½ lb)
250 g	9 oz
275 g	10 oz
300 g	11 oz
325-350 g	12 oz
375 g	13 oz
400 g	14 oz
425 g	15 oz
450 g	16 oz (1 lb)
500 g	17 ½ oz (½ kg)
1 kg	2.2 lb
1.5 kg	3.3 lb
2 kg	4.4 lb

VOLUME

METRIC	IMPERIAL
25 ml	1 fl oz
50 ml	2 fl oz
75 ml	3 fl oz
100 ml	4 fl oz
150 ml	5 fl oz (¼ pt)
200 ml	7 fl oz
250 ml	8 fl oz (1 cup)
300 ml	10 fl oz (½ pt)
350 ml	12 fl oz
400 ml	14 fl oz
450 ml	15 fl oz (¾ pt)
500 ml	18 fl oz
600 ml	20 fl oz (1 pt)
750 ml	25 fl oz (1¼ pt)
900 ml	30 fl oz (1½ pt)
1 litre	35 fl oz (1¾ pt)

LENGTH

METRIC	IMPERIAL
3 mm	⅛ in
5 mm	¼ in
10 mm (1 cm)	½ in
2 cm	¾ in
2.5 cm	1 in
3 cm	1¼ in
4 cm	1½ in
4.5 cm	1¾ in
5 cm	2 in
10 cm	4 in
20.5 cm	8 in
30.5 cm	12 in (1 ft)
91.5 cm	36 in (1 yd)
100 cm (1 m)	39 in

INTRODUCTION

Cooking is all about pleasure. The excitement of discovering a bounty of fresh products. The fun of combining these to produce mouth-watering dishes. The stimulation of new tastes, textures and flavours. And finally the joy of sharing with family and friends a lovingly prepared and carefully presented meal. For me there is no activity more rewarding and few that can be such fun. *The Daily Express All Colour Cookery Book* provides the opportunity for me to share this enjoyment with you.

Being Executive Chef at The Dorchester Hotel in London is a unique experience. For me, it represents the culmination of 20 years of devotion to food. However, with 7 kitchens and over 110 chefs to supervise, cooking at work takes on a totally different perspective from preparing meals at home.

At home, cooking is a relaxing hobby. Here I enjoy raiding the refrigerator, or shopping at our local shops and market to select the freshest ingredients in season. Back at home, in my kitchen, I then experiment with these to produce dishes that we enjoy as a family or when entertaining.

The successful results of these experiments are the recipes which were originally published in *The Daily Express* and which I now have pleasure in presenting in full colour in this book. They are not the recipes which we serve at The Dorchester, where I have only the very finest, and therefore most expensive ingredients to hand, not to mention a brigade of professional helpers with a range of skills and equipment that any chef would envy. No - these recipes are from my personal files, developed at home. I have taken into account the confines of a domestic kitchen and equipment, not to mention limited time and budget. They are not necessarily fashionable or trendy recipes, but each one is absolutely delicious.

The recipes in this book are aimed at the domestic cook - not the professional - who shares my enjoyment of transforming everyday ingredients into exciting dishes that please both the eye and the palate. The home cook will have no difficulty in producing any of them, from the simplest to the most sophisticated.

The book contains much more than recipes. I have also included some valuable tips on buying, storing and preparing the various ingredients, to help you to take advantage of products at their peak throughout the year. This follows my basic philosophy of cooking - one that I apply both at work and at home - that the result can only be as good as the ingredients used. Nothing can compare with fresh products in season: perfectly formed, picked at their peak and succulent in flavour. But to take advantage of this principle you have to know some fundamental details about the products you use, and this is what I have provided here.

The recipes have been reproduced in *The Daily Express All Colour Cookery Book* in the order in which they were printed in *The Daily Express* to present you with an alternative and, in my experience, highly successful approach to cooking, where the ingredients take priority over the preconceived formula of menu planning.

In reproducing the recipes for this book, I have taken into consideration the many helpful comments that I have received from *Daily Express* readers. Each recipe has also been tested twice: first by a chef and then by someone who is not a professional cook, preparing the food in their own kitchen at home.

To assist you, we have provided both metric and imperial measurements for all the recipes. But please remember to choose one or the other, and never change over half way through a recipe. This may jeopardise the end result.

In view of the current preoccupation with health, and, for some of us, with our waist-lines, each recipe also gives an approximate calorie content. This is only intended to assist those of you who are following a calorie controlled diet.

All the pictures in this book were taken as a result of the dishes being tested. They are pictures of real food taken in a real kitchen! In other words they were not "styled" in a studio, but show you exactly the results that you too can achieve at home.

Everyday cooking can easily become rather repetitive, but there is no reason why it should stay that way. Thanks to the unprecedented availability of fresh ingredients and the advance in simple domestic equipment, everyone is now able to enjoy the adventure of using new ingredients. It seems as if unusual, exotic and previously unobtainable foods are gaining familiarity on almost a daily basis. A sense of adventure and a love of good food can transform these ingredients into delicious meals for a range of occasions, from family lunches or suppers to dinner parties and other special occasions.

The compilation of these recipes has provided endless hours of enjoyment - even a few of exasperation - but certainly lots of fun! I believe that the resulting collection of recipes will provide you with both pleasure and inspiration.

I hope that this book will encourage you to experiment through the year, and that you, your family and friends will enjoy many happy meals together. Good luck!

Willi Elsener

HALIBUT

Halibut is a flat fish, similar in appearance to turbot with dark olive skin. It can grow to a great size, weighing in at anything from 9 lb-400 lb (4-180 kg). Because it is such a large fish, it is seldom seen whole and is generally sold in steaks, cutlets or fillets. Available all year, it is at its best from August to April.

The firm, white flesh should be quite dry and requires careful cooking, but, with the right treatment, has an excellent flavour. In fact, halibut, like turbot, is regarded as one of the best quality fish.

When purchasing halibut, as with any fish, make sure that the flesh is firm - a watery appearance is an indication of staleness. Preferably use on the day of purchase, or store well covered in the refrigerator for up to two days.

Any recipe for cod or turbot would be suitable for halibut, which is usually served baked or grilled.

For a change, though, serve poached halibut with salad in a light vinaigrette, or try it in a stew or fish pie or marinated in olive oil and herbs and grilled.

Alternatively, halibut can be cooked simply wrapped in greaseproof paper with some vegetables and baked in the oven.

The following recipes call for halibut, but cod or turbot may be used instead if you prefer.

Halibut Steaks with a Sesame Seed Crust and Pepper Sauce

Serves 2

CALORIES
Approximately 360 per portion

INGREDIENTS:

FISH
2 halibut steaks
1 tsp light soya sauce
1 tsp vegetable oil

SAUCE

1 tbsp vegetable oil
1 tsp finely chopped shallot or onion
½ clove garlic, peeled and crushed
2 yellow peppers, deseeded and diced
2 fl oz/50 ml dry white wine
8 fl oz/250 ml fish or vegetable stock
salt & freshly ground white pepper

HERB CRUST
1 oz/25 g breadcrumbs, preferably brioche
1 tsp each fresh parsley and coriander leaves
1 tsp roasted sesame seeds
2 tsp unsalted butter

OVEN TEMPERATURE
200°C/400°F/Gas Mark 6

METHOD:

SAUCE
Heat the vegetable oil and gently sweat the shallots and garlic until transparent, but without colouring. Add the peppers and continue to sweat. Add the white wine and reduce to half the quantity.

Add the stock, cover with a lid and continue to cook until the peppers are tender. Season and liquidise in a food processor. Pass through a fine sieve into a saucepan and keep aside.

FISH
Marinate the halibut in the soya sauce and season. Heat the oil in a non-stick pan and lightly brown the steaks. Place in an oven-proof dish and bake in the oven for about 10 minutes.

HERB CRUST
Blend the breadcrumbs and herbs in a blender until fine. Add the sesame seeds. Keep aside.

TO FINISH OFF
Remove the halibut from oven and brush lightly with the butter. Cover with the breadcrumb mixture and brown under the grill. Serve immediately. Serve the pepper sauce separately.

POACHING TIP

Poaching is an important basic cooking method to keep fish moist and tender. It does not mean boiling or simmering. In poaching, cooking liquid should be kept just below simmering point. Poach in water, with some white wine or vinegar, a piece of onion, celery or the white part of a leek, salt, a bay leaf and some peppercorns and cloves.

Halibut Steaks with a Sesame Seed Crust and Pepper Sauce

Fillet of Halibut with Guinness and Pommery Mustard Sauce

Serves 4

CALORIES
Approximately 610 per portion

INGREDIENTS
2 tbsp vegetable oil
4 halibut fillets or steaks
salt & freshly ground white pepper

SAUCE
1 tsp flour
2 oz/50 g butter, room temperature
1 shallot or ¼ onion, peeled and finely chopped
2 fl oz/50 ml Guinness
7 fl oz/200 ml fish stock
1 tsp Pommery or grain mustard
2 oz/50 g unsalted butter, cut into cubes
parsley and chives, finely chopped, to garnish

OVEN TEMPERATURE
350°F/180°C/Gas Mark 4

METHOD:

SAUCE
Whisk the butter until soft and add the flour. Keep aside.

Mix the shallots and Guinness in a saucepan. Bring to the boil and reduce to half the quantity. Add the fish stock and reduce to half the quantity. Keep aside.

FISH
Heat the oil in a non-stick pan. Fry the seasoned halibut steaks on both sides until golden brown.

Place in an oven-proof dish and bake for about 10 minutes until cooked but still moist.

TO FINISH OFF
Bring the sauce to the boil. Add the butter and flour mixture and boil for 3-4 minutes. Remove from the heat, add the mustard and whisk in the butter cubes. Season. Pour the sauce over the fish, garnish with the chopped herbs and serve.

CHICKEN

Chicken is one of the most popular and reasonably priced meals in Britain. Chicken, both fresh and frozen, lends itself to so many ways of cooking and blends with such a wide variety of flavours.

Most of the chickens that we eat today are specially reared, but free-range chickens are available, at a price. The flavour of a chicken will depend on its age and what it has been fed. Younger birds have tender, mild-tasting flesh, whereas older fowls have a more developed flavour. Chickens are usually sold according to age and size.

Poussins are baby chickens, 4-6 weeks old, weighing up to 1 lb (450 g). They are suitable for grilling or roasting. Allow one per person.

Double poussin are 6-10 weeks old and weigh about 2 1b (900 g). They are suitable for cooking in the same way as individual poussins, but they will feed two people.

Spring chickens are about 6 weeks old and average 2½ 1b (1.1 kg). They are best roasted to serve three or four.

Roasting (or broiling) chickens are usually over 31b (1.3 kg) and up to one year old. They make the most popular choice for a family meal. These birds are also sold jointed, and are therefore ideal for grilling, boiling or casseroling.

Boiling fowls are less often available. They are older birds that have already laid eggs. As they tend to be meaty, they require more cooking time, and are ideal for casseroles.

My recipes call for chicken joints, which can be purchased, but it is more economical to buy whole birds, joint them and use the bones for home-made stock in soup or sauce.

Chicken Legs with an Orange Pepper Sauce

Serves 4

CALORIES
Approximately 600 calories per portion

INGREDIENTS
2 tbsp vegetable oil
4 chicken leg joints (thigh and drumstick)
salt & freshly ground white pepper
flour to dust chicken

SAUCE
2 tbsp vegetable oil
1 shallot or ¼ onion, peeled and finely chopped
1 clove garlic, peeled and crushed
1 red pepper, deseeded, cut into cubes
1 green pepper, deseeded, cut into cubes
juice of 1 orange
1 tsp mild paprika powder
5 fl oz/150 ml chicken stock
(reserve 2 fl oz/50 ml to dissolve cornflour)
7 fl oz/200 ml single cream
2 tbsp cornflour

GARNISH
your choice of herbs
red and green pepper cubes reserved from above and blanched for 3 minutes

OVEN TEMPERATURE
180°C/350°F/Gas Mark 4

METHOD
Season the chicken pieces and dust with flour. Heat the oil in a non-stick pan and brown the chicken. Remove and place in a fairly large oven-proof dish. Bake in the oven for 10 minutes.

In the meantime, prepare the sauce. Sweat the shallots or onion and the garlic in the oil in a saucepan. Add the red and green pepper cubes, reserving 1 tbsp of each for the garnish, and sweat for a minute.

Add the orange juice and bring to the boil. Add the paprika and stock and bring to the boil.

Pour the sauce over the chicken. Cover with a lid and return to the oven for another 20 minutes. Pierce the thickest part of the chicken leg to check if the legs are cooked.

TO FINISH OFF
Remove the chicken legs from the sauce and keep warm in a serving dish.

Pour the sauce into a pan and add the cream. Boil for about 3 minutes. Skim off the fat and season.

Dissolve the cornflour in the reserved chicken stock, add to the sauce and bring to the boil. Pour over the chicken legs. Garnish with the blanched pepper cubes and herbs of your choice.

Chicken Legs with an Orange Pepper Sauce (left) & Glazed Chicken Breast with a Lemon and Mushroom Sauce (right)

Glazed Chicken Breast with a Lemon and Mushroom Sauce

Serves 2

CALORIES
Approximately 550 per portion

INGREDIENTS
3 tbsp vegetable oil
2 chicken breasts, each about 6 oz/175 g

MARINADE
salt & freshly ground white pepper
pinch ground ginger
2 tsp light soya sauce
4 tsp dry sherry
pinch English mustard powder

SAUCE
1 oz/25 g butter
2 oz/50 g button mushrooms
7 fl oz/200 ml single cream
½ tsp lemon zest
1 egg yolk, lightly beaten

METHOD
Mix together all the marinade ingredients. Pour over the chicken breasts and marinate for about 30 minutes. Drain, and reserve the marinade for the sauce.

Heat the oil in a non-stick pan and fry the breasts until they are brown on both sides. Place in an oven-proof dish and keep warm.

SAUCE
Heat the butter in a saucepan, add the mushrooms and brown slightly.

Add the marinade and bring to the boil. Add the cream and boil until a creamy consistency is obtained. Add the lemon zest. Season with salt and pepper.

Leave to cool, then add the egg yolk. Pour the sauce over the chicken breasts and brown under the grill on the highest heat.

> **TO TEST COOKED CHICKEN**
> To test that your chicken is cooked, use a skewer and pierce the thickest part of the chicken - e.g. the thigh. The juices will run clear when the bird is ready for eating.

PORK

Over recent years pork has gained in popularity. However, not all that long ago pork was only sold during the winter months, due to its poor keeping qualities. Refrigeration and modern breeding methods have, of course, helped to overcome this.

Good quality pork has whitish-pink, fine textured flesh with a fair proportion of fat and no smell. Avoid joints that look grey and moist with soft, oily fat: this leads to excessive moisture loss during cooking and a poor flavour. The skin or rind should be thin, smooth and free from any hairs. Thick, coarse rind indicates that the meat is from an older pig.

Pork is highly nutritious - a good source of protein and vitamin B. But remember that pork meat must always be well cooked before serving.

If you plan to roast the joint, ensure that the rind is well scored, not only to let the heat through and aid cooking, but also for ease of carving. Pork joints are most commonly roasted and served with the traditional accompaniments of herb forcemeat balls and apple sauce or jelly. However, pork is also excellent salted and boiled, cut into chops or ribs and marinated for grilling or frying, or pot-roasted.

Braised Pork and Cabbage Parcels

Serves 4

CALORIES
Approximately 330 per portion

INGREDIENTS
1 cabbage, medium size
½ onion, peeled and finely chopped
1 lb/450 g pork sausage meat
½ tsp sage
1 tbsp breadcrumbs
1 tsp grain mustard
4 fl oz/100 ml chicken stock
butter to grease an oven-proof dish

OVEN TEMPERATURE
180°C/350°F/Gas Mark 4

METHOD

Remove the leaves from the cabbage very carefully and use 12 large ones for this recipe. Cut out the stems with a knife.

Cook the leaves in boiling, salted water for about 5 minutes. Refresh in iced water and drain. Keep the leaves aside.

FILLING

Boil the onion in salted water for about 30 seconds. Rinse in cold water and drain. Mix the onion thoroughly with the sage, sausage meat, breadcrumbs and mustard. Season with salt and pepper.

Divide the mixture into 12 equal portions.

FORMING THE PARCEL

Place the whole cabbage leaves one at a time flat on a piece of paper kitchen towel in front of you.
Place the filling in the shape of a sausage about 1½ in/4 cm long on top of the cabbage leaf. Fold in both sides and roll it to the shape of a sausage. Do the same with the other leaves and the rest of the filling.

TO FINISH OFF

Butter an oven-proof dish and place the cabbage parcels next to each other in it. Bring the stock to the boil and pour over the parcels. Bake in the oven for about 30 minutes (baste in the juices once or twice during cooking) and then serve.

POT-ROASTING

Pot-roasting is an ideal method of cooking for many cuts of pork. Try this with a boneless neck or shoulder. Place the meat in a pan with a little butter. Cover and roast in the oven at 150°C/300°F/Gas Mark 1, basting regularly, until three-quarters cooked. Uncover, increase the heat to 180°C/350°F/Gas Mark 4 and cook until golden brown. Remove the meat. Add wine to the cooking liquid and boil until reduced to half. Strain, then season, and serve with the roast.

Braised Pork and Cabbage Parcels (top) & Pork Chops with a Pepperonata (below)

Pork Chops with a Pepperonata

Serves 2

CALORIES
Approximately 325 per portion

INGREDIENTS
1 tbsp vegetable oil
2 pork chops

SAUCE
1 tbsp vegetable oil
½ onion, peeled and chopped
½ clove garlic, peeled and crushed
1 yellow pepper, halved and diced
1 red pepper, halved and diced
1 tsp tomato puree
1 tomato, peeled, deseeded and diced
4 fl oz/100 ml vegetable stock
pinch of rosemary and ginger powder
salt & freshly ground pepper

METHOD:

SAUCE
Heat the oil in a saucepan. Add the onion and garlic and sweat until transparent but without colouring.

Add the diced peppers and sweat for 1 minute. Add the tomato puree and cook for a further minute. Add the diced tomato, rosemary, ginger and vegetable stock.

Bring to the boil until the peppers are cooked but still a little crisp. Season and keep aside.

TO FINISH OFF
Brush the pork chops with oil. Grill the pork chops on both sides until golden brown. Season with salt and pepper.
Place in a serving dish and pour the hot pepperonata on top.

HADDOCK

Haddock is a large, round fish of the cod family. It is easily recognised by the dark markings behind the gills and the lines that run down each side of the body. The flesh is firm, tender and white with a mild and pleasing flavour.

Haddock is available all year through, but best between November and February. It is sold whole or in fillets, cutlets or steaks. The fish can also be bought smoked. Smoked haddock should be a pale yellow colour. Avoid any that is very bright yellow - this has probably been artificially coloured and will have a poor flavour.

Most often it is the larger fish which are filleted and smoked, but the most famous of smoked haddock are Finnan Haddock. These are smaller fish, usually 1-3 lb (450 g-1.3 kg), which are split and smoked on the bone. Very small fish which have been filleted and smoked are known as golden cutlets. Haddock may also be bought as Arbroath Smokies. These are small fish which are smoked whole until brown in colour. Try the different types available: they are all delicious, but one may appeal to your taste buds more than another.

Fresh haddock is suitable for baking, grilling, frying or poaching. As with all fish, avoid over-cooking, which will dry out the tender, white flesh. Smoked haddock dries out particularly easily when cooked. To avoid this, always poach covered with liquid.

Haddock with a Mustard Sauce

Serves 4

CALORIES
Approximately 330 per portion

INGREDIENTS
4 haddock fillets
salt & freshly ground white pepper
1 tbsp butter or vegetable oil
½ small onion, peeled and finely chopped
4 fl oz/100 ml dry white wine
4 fl oz/100 ml fish stock

SAUCE
4 fl oz/100 ml cooking liquid from above
8 fl oz/250 ml single cream
½ tbsp butter, room temperature
½ tbsp flour
1½ tsp grain mustard
juice of half a lemon
salt & freshly ground pepper

GARNISH
your choice of herbs

METHOD
Season the fish fillets with salt and pepper.

Heat a pan large enough to accommodate the 4 fillets. Melt the butter, add the onion and sweat until transparent but without colouring. Add the wine and fish stock and bring to the boil.

Reduce the heat and add the haddock fillets. Cover with a lid and simmer very gently for about 10 minutes.

Remove the fish, place in a serving dish and keep warm in the oven.

SAUCE
Strain the required amount of cooking liquid into a small saucepan and bring to the boil (freeze the remainder for use in other fish sauces). Add the cream and boil gently.
Mix the flour and butter with a fork into a paste (Beurre Manié). Add the paste to the sauce using a whisk and simmer for 2-3 minutes, stirring constantly, until the sauce has a creamy consistency.
Remove from the heat and add the mustard and lemon juice. Season with salt and pepper.

TO FINISH OFF
Remove the serving dish from the oven and pour the sauce over the fish. Garnish with herbs and serve.

> POACHING HADDOCK
> Various methods can be used to poach smoked haddock. My preferred method, which keeps the delicate flavour without drying out the flesh, is as follows. Bring sufficient milk and water to cover the fish to the boil. Lay the fish in a flat dish and pour over the boiling liquid. Cover with a lid for 10 minutes. The fish will be cooked and deliciously tender.

Haddock Fillets with a Basilic and Pine Kernel Sauce

Serves 4

CALORIES
Approximately 340 per portion

INGREDIENTS
4 haddock fillets, no skin
salt & freshly ground pepper
14 fl oz/400 ml fish stock

SAUCE
1 tbsp pine kernels
1 tsp basil leaves, finely chopped
2 tsp parsley, finely chopped
1 clove garlic, crushed and finely chopped
2 tbsp grated Parmesan cheese
3 fl oz/75 ml olive or vegetable oil
3 tbsp fish stock from above
salt & freshly ground pepper

GARNISH
black olives
1 tomato, peeled, deseeded and diced

METHOD:

SAUCE
Roast the pine kernels under the grill until golden brown. Leave to cool and chop very finely. Place in a bowl. Add the chopped basil and parsley and the garlic. Add the grated Parmesan. Add the olive oil and mix thoroughly.

FISH
Season the fish fillets. Boil the fish stock in a pan large enough to hold the 4 fish fillets. Place the fish fillets in the cooking liquid, reduce the heat to simmering point, cover with a lid and simmer very gently for about 10 minutes until cooked. Remove from the cooking liquid and place on a serving dish. Keep warm in the oven.

Pass the cooking liquid through a sieve into a bowl and reserve 2 tbsp for the sauce. Freeze the remainder of the stock for use in other fish sauces.

TO FINISH OFF
Add the cold cooking liquid to the sauce and stir. Season with salt and freshly ground pepper.

Remove the fish from the oven, spoon the sauce over and garnish with tomato and black olives.

Lemon can be served with this dish.

BEEF

Britain has long been thought of as a country with a healthy appetite for roast beef and this still remains something of a national dish. However, we are not such high consumers of beef as we used to be.

This is partially due to the rise in health consciousness, but despite this, a delicious beef joint or hearty beef casserole is still a meal to be savoured. Meat is an important part of our diet and it supplies us with minerals, protein and vitamins.

The best beef comes from younger animals. This is matured, or "hung", to tenderise the meat. On properly hung beef the meat should be dark red and moist with creamy yellow fat. Meat that is very bright red indicates beef that has not hung sufficiently and therefore is not tender. Meat that is over dark and sinewy indicates cuts from an older animal and is likely to be tough.

Quality beef should also have a good covering of fat and be well marbled with flecks of fat throughout. This will help to keep the meat moist and tender whilst cooking. Avoid meat with a line of gristle between lean and fat, as this usually suggests that the meat is from an old animal.

Cuts of beef and the names by which they're known vary across the country. As do the prices. But remember, inexpensive cuts are just as nutritious as the most expensive ones - and, with the correct preparation, very tasty too.

Oriental Beef Casserole

Serves 4

CALORIES
Approximately 320 per portion

INGREDIENTS
1 tbsp vegetable oil
2 braising steaks, about 6 oz/150 g each
1 onion, peeled and finely chopped
1 tbsp cornstarch
2 fl oz/50 ml cold water

MARINADE
2 tbsp light soya sauce
2 fl oz/50 ml sherry
1 tbsp brown sugar
pinch grated ginger or ground ginger
1 clove garlic, peeled and crushed
14 fl oz/400 ml beef stock
pinch chilli powder
freshly ground pepper

GARNISH (OPTIONAL)
1 tsp vegetable oil
4 oz/100 g beansprouts
1 red pepper, cut into fine strips
coriander leaves

OVEN TEMPERATURE
180°C/350°F/Gas Mark 4

METHOD
Preferably the night before cooking the casserole, mix together in a large bowl the soya sauce, sherry, brown sugar, ginger, garlic, beef stock, chilli and pepper to make a marinade.

Add the braising steak and cover with clingfilm. Refrigerate overnight.

Remove the meat from the marinade and dry on a kitchen towel. Keep the marinade to one side.

Heat the oil in a non-stick pan and brown the steaks on both sides on medium heat. Remove the steaks from the pan and place in a casserole dish. Use the remaining oil in the pan to sweat the onions until transparent, but without colouring.

Add the marinade and bring to the boil. Add the meat. Cover the casserole dish with a lid and simmer for about 2 hours in the oven until the meat is tender, adding water if necessary.

Remove the steaks from the casserole, place in a serving dish and keep warm.

TO FINISH OFF
Mix together the cornstarch and the cold water. Add to the sauce, bring to the boil and cook for 2-3 minutes. Adjust the seasoning if necessary.

Pass through a sieve and pour over the steaks.

Heat the oil in a non-stick pan and add the beansprouts and strips of pepper. Stir-fry for 1 minute, season with salt and pepper and use to garnish the meat. Sprinkle with coriander leaves.

Steak with a Mushroom and Gherkin Sauce

Serves 2

CALORIES
Approximately 630 per portion

INGREDIENTS
1 tbsp vegetable oil
2 steaks (your choice of rump, sirloin, fillet)
salt & freshly ground white pepper

SAUCE
1 tbsp vegetable oil
1 shallot or ¼ onion, peeled and finely chopped
2 oz/50 g button mushrooms, sliced
2 gherkins, cut into strips ¾ in/2 cm long
2 fl oz/50 ml white wine
4 fl oz/100 ml beef stock
8 fl oz/250 ml single cream
1 tbsp grain mustard
Worcester sauce
1 tsp parsley, chopped
salt & freshly ground white pepper

METHOD
Season the steaks with salt and pepper. Heat the oil in a non-stick pan and brown the steak on both sides. Reduce the heat and cook to the required degree. Remove from the pan and keep warm in a serving dish.

SAUCE
Using the same pan, heat the oil, add the shallots or onion and sweat without colouring until transparent.

Add the mushrooms and gherkin. Add the wine and bring to the boil. Add the stock and boil. Reduce to half the quantity.

Add the cream and simmer until a creamy consistency is obtained. Remove from the heat and whisk in the mustard.

Season with Worcester sauce, salt and pepper as required. Add the parsley.

Cover the steaks with the sauce, or serve the sauce separately.

STORING MEAT
The ideal storage temperature for fresh meat is 1°C. If you do not have sophisticated refrigeration, make sure that you place your meat on the bottom shelf of your refrigerator on a tray covered with clingfilm. Try to use it within 2-3 days of purchase. You can enhance the flavour by marinating it in some vegetable oil and herbs.

CAULIFLOWER

Cauliflower makes a welcome addition to any dish, and, with a little imagination, it makes a tasty meal in itself. Although it is available throughout the year, there is a distinct difference between the true summer and winter varieties. On summer cauliflowers the dark green leaves open outwards, whereas on the winter varieties they turn protectively inwards.

When choosing, whatever the season, look for a creamy white head, not quite fully developed, with clean white stalks. Avoid any with limp leaves and loose, damaged or browning heads.

To prepare, either leave whole, removing only the coarse outer leaves, or divide into 6-8 florets. If cooking whole, cut a cross in the thick stem. A whole medium-sized cauliflower will require 10-15 minutes cooking in fast-boiling, salted water; florets will only need 5-8 minutes. Florets can then be reassembled into their original shape for serving if desired.

In addition to that perennial favourite, cauliflower cheese, try cauliflower served with a spicy tomato sauce (laced with garlic if that's to your taste). Or cook the cauliflower in the usual way, then serve topped with breadcrumbs and almond flakes tossed in garlic herb butter.

For a hearty family dish, try curried cauliflower or layer a casserole with creamed spinach, cauliflower, home-made tomato sauce and top with cheese sauce. Diced ham or bacon makes a tasty addition too.

Alternatively, cauliflower is quite delicious in a salad, broken into small florets and served raw or very lightly blanched. Try them dunked in your favourite dip or tossed in a spicy dressing.

Cauliflower Gratin with Walnuts

Serves 4

CALORIES
Approximately 260 per portion

INGREDIENTS
1 medium cauliflower

SAUCE
2 tbsp oil
1 shallot or ¼ onion, peeled and finely chopped
1 clove garlic, peeled and crushed
1½ oz/40 g flour
4 fl oz/100 ml white wine
14 fl oz/400 ml vegetable stock
4 fl oz/100 ml single cream
salt & freshly ground white pepper

TOPPING
2 tbsp walnuts, finely chopped
1 tbsp breadcrumbs
1 tsp fresh parsley, chopped
2 eggs, hard-boiled and finely chopped
Parmesan or Cheddar cheese, grated

OVEN TEMPERATURE
200°C/400°F/Gas Mark 6

METHOD

Remove the green leaves from the cauliflower and clean. Remove the stalk and break the florets into equal-sized pieces.

Cook in boiling salted water until tender but still crisp. Refresh under cold water and drain.

Place the florets next to each other in an ovenproof dish and keep aside.

SAUCE

Heat the oil in a saucepan. Add the shallots or onion and the garlic and sweat until transparent, but without colouring. Add the flour and mix until it is absorbed in the oil. Remove from the heat.

Add the white wine and one third of the cold vegetable stock. Bring to the boil, stirring constantly.

Add the remaining stock and the cream and simmer for 10-15 minutes. Season, then pass through a fine sieve. Pour the sauce over the cauliflower florets, making sure that they are all covered.

TO FINISH OFF

Mix together the walnuts, breadcrumbs, parsley, egg and cheese and sprinkle over the cauliflower.

Bake in the oven for about 20-25 minutes until golden brown.

Cauliflower Gratin with Walnuts

Curried Cauliflower and Mushroom Soup

Serves 4

CALORIES
Approximately 175 per portion

INGREDIENTS
3 tbsp vegetable oil

1 onion, medium size, peeled and finely chopped

½ clove garlic, peeled and crushed

1 lb/450 g cauliflower florets, roughly chopped

2 tsp mild curry powder

1 medium tomato, peeled, deseeded and roughly diced

4 oz/100 g button mushrooms, sliced

½ oz/15 g wholemeal plain flour

2 pt/1.5 ltr vegetable stock

salt & freshly ground pepper

GARNISH
2 oz/50 g button mushrooms, sliced

1 oz/25 g roasted sesame seeds

OVEN TEMPERATURE
Grill on highest heat

METHOD

Heat the vegetable oil in a saucepan. Add the onion and garlic and sweat until transparent, but without colouring.

Add the cauliflower florets and curry powder. Then cook for about 1 minute on a medium heat before adding the tomato and mushrooms.

Add the flour and stir. Add the vegetable stock and bring to the boil. Stir and simmer, covered, for about 35 minutes until the cauliflower is tender.

Place in a blender and blend until the mixture is smooth. Return to the saucepan and reheat.

If the soup is too thick, add some vegetable stock or water. Season with salt and freshly ground pepper.

To garnish, add sliced mushrooms and bring to the boil. Sprinkle with sesame seeds.

If desired, serve with plain yoghurt.

PREPARING CAULIFLOWER

Bugs find it easy to hide in the crevices of cauliflowers and similar varieties of vegetables. Before cooking your cauliflower, remove the leaves, preferably break into florets, then soak in cold, salted water.

This will ensure that you don't have any strangers sharing your meal!

SPINACH

Popeye had the right idea when he ate lots of spinach! It is delicious, full of vitamins and minerals and very low in calories.

Generally obtainable all year through, with the best on sale in March and April, there are three varieties: the round-leaved summer variety, the prickly-leaved winter variety and spinach beet, which, although quite tasty, is not a fine spinach and is seldom seen on sale in the shops.

When buying, check loose leaves for a good green colour - discard any that are yellowing or have hard stalks or flowering shoots. If the spinach is pre-packaged, check carefully before purchasing, as the wrapping may cause the leaves to sweat. The tender, dark leaves bruise easily, so need to be handled with care. They also wilt quickly, so are best stored in a jug of water in the fridge until used. Preferably eat within two days of purchase.

Early recipe journals used to report that spinach was best eaten raw - today this still holds true. To benefit fully from all the nutrients in spinach, serve young leaves, either on their own or tossed with other leaves, to make a hearty salad with crisp bacon, ham, a poached egg or diced cheese.

Alternatively, serve older leaves warm, cooked in a pan with no water added, then flavoured with a hint of nutmeg. Or chopped and mixed with tomatoes, onions, garlic and a hint of curry. Or sweated in hot oil and tossed with avocado and bacon.

For a luxurious accompaniment to roast lamb or beef, try gratinated spinach, or serve it with a slice of ham and an egg.

Gratinated Spinach (left) & Spinach and Smoked Haddock Pie (right)

Gratinated Spinach

Serves 4

CALORIES
Approximately 350 per portion

INGREDIENTS
3.3 lb/1.5 kg spinach, washed with stems removed
½ oz/15 g butter or vegetable oil
1 shallot or ¼ onion, peeled and finely chopped

SAUCE
1 fl oz/25 ml vegetable oil
1½ oz/40 g flour
10 fl oz/300 ml milk
7 fl oz/200 ml cream
salt & freshly ground pepper
nutmeg
Parmesan cheese, grated

OVEN TEMPERATURE
200°C/400°F/Gas Mark 6

METHOD:

SPINACH

Cook the spinach in boiling, salted water for about 5 minutes. Remove spinach and refresh in cold water.

Drain and press between two plates to remove any excess water. Keep the spinach aside. Heat the butter in a saucepan and sweat shallots until transparent, but without colouring. Cool and keep aside.

SAUCE

Heat oil in a saucepan and stir in the flour. Add the milk and cream and bring to the boil stirring constantly. Reduce heat and simmer for 10 minutes. Season with salt and ground pepper. Add grated nutmeg to taste.

TO FINISH OFF

Mix one third of the sauce with the cooked spinach and shallots, making sure that all the ingredients are well mixed. The mixture should not be runny. Season with salt and pepper. Place the mixture in an ovenproof dish. Pour the remaining sauce evenly on top. Sprinkle with Parmesan, bake in the oven for about 20 minutes and serve.

Spinach and Smoked Haddock Pie

Serves 2

CALORIES
Approximately 870 per portion.

INGREDIENTS
12 oz/350 g spinach, washed with stems removed
5 oz/150 g smoked haddock
8 fl oz/250 ml milk
1 egg (for eggwash)

SAUCE
3 oz/75 g butter, soft
1 tbsp flour
1 tbsp vegetable oil
1 shallot or ¼ onion, peeled and finely chopped
½ clove garlic, peeled and crushed
5 fl oz/150 ml white wine
8 fl oz/250 ml cooking liquid from above
salt & freshly ground pepper
14 oz/400 g potato, mashed

OVEN TEMPERATURE
200°C/400°F/Gas Mark 6

METHOD

Pre-heat the oven. Cook the spinach in salted water for 5 minutes. Refresh and keep aside. Poach the haddock in milk until cooked. Reserve the cooking liquid for the sauce. Flake the haddock and keep aside.

SAUCE

In a bowl, using a wooden spoon, mix the butter and flour until smooth and keep aside. Heat the vegetable oil in a saucepan. Sweat the shallot or onion and garlic until transparent but without colouring. Add the white wine and boil until it is reduced by half. Add the reserved cooking liquid and bring to the boil. Add the butter and flour mixture. Boil for 5 minutes, season and strain through a sieve into a saucepan.

TO FINISH OFF

Mix the spinach and sauce together. Gently add the cooked haddock. Place in a pie dish, pipe mashed potatoes on top and brush with eggwash. Bake for 30 minutes in the oven.

DRAINING COOKED SPINACH

Spinach soaks up lots of water when boiled and needs to be drained well. To do this, squeeze out excess water by pressing between two plates. Reserve the juices, which contain lost nutrients, for adding to a sauce or gravy.

PRAWNS

There's something rather special about prawns. They always conjure up images of sunny seaside holidays for me, but, of course, they can be enjoyed all year through - and, even without the sun and sea, they still taste delicious.

There are many different varieties of prawns, which differ widely in size. The most commonly available are those which are small, soft-shelled and grey, turning pink when cooked. These are usually sold pre-boiled, with or without shells, and are ideal for use cold in salads, sandwiches and soups, or in prepared dishes. If reheating, remember that they are already cooked, and, being delicate, will toughen easily, so always add them to hot dishes at the last minute.

Larger varieties are better suited to hot dishes. They're also ideal for hors d'oeuvres and garnishes, and are quite superb on their own. The largest of the British prawns is the Dublin Bay variety, about 4 inches (10 cm) long, and pale pink when cooked. These are sold either cooked or raw, with or without shells, fresh or frozen.

There are also many varieties imported from overseas and sold frozen, invariably cooked and shelled. If you're looking for large prawns, the Pacific or Mediterranean varieties are a good buy and are often found shelled, raw and frozen - ideal for including in hot dishes. Allow them to thaw completely before using.

For a main meal, allow 1 lb (450 g) unshelled or 8 oz (225 g) shelled, small prawns per person or 6-10 large prawns. They are delicious simply boiled and served cold with a tasty sauce, or grilled or pan-fried in butter.

Prawns with Passion Fruit and Chilli Sauce

Serves 4

CALORIES
Approximately 300 per portion

INGREDIENTS
24 large raw prawns (heads removed)
1 oz/25 g butter, unsalted

SAUCE
1 tbsp vegetable oil
prawn shells (from above)
1 shallot or ¼ onion, peeled and finely chopped
½ clove garlic
4 fl oz/100 ml dry white wine
7 fl oz/200 ml fish stock
7 fl oz/200 ml double cream
1 passion fruit, pulp only
1 chilli, chopped, seeds removed
salt & freshly ground white pepper

GARNISH
fresh coriander leaves

METHOD
Peel and clean the prawns, keeping the shells to one side.

SAUCE
Heat the oil in a saucepan, add the prawn shells and sauté for 2 minutes.

Reduce heat, add the shallots or onion and the garlic. Sweat for a further minute without colouring.

Add white wine and reduce to half the quantity. Add fish stock and reduce to half the quantity.

Add double cream, reduce to sauce consistency, stirring constantly, then pass through a sieve. Bring to the boil and add the passion fruit pulp.

Add chopped chilli to taste and season. Keep to one side.

TO FINISH OFF
Season prawns with salt and pepper.

Heat butter in a non-stick pan, add prawns and pan-fry until golden brown (they should be cooked but still moist inside).

Place in the centre of a dish.

Heat the sauce and pour around the prawns. Garnish with coriander leaves.

Spicy Prawns with Tomato and Herbs

Serves 2

CALORIES
Approximately 205 per portion

INGREDIENTS
12 large fresh prawns, peeled and veins
removed (or frozen and thawed before use)

1 tbsp olive or vegetable oil

1 shallot or ¼ onion, peeled and finely
chopped

1 clove garlic

1 small chilli, chopped, seeds removed

SAUCE
1 tbsp olive or vegetable oil

1 small green pepper, cut into
cubes ½ in (1 cm) square

3 large tomatoes, peeled, deseeded and
coarsely chopped (reserve 2 tbsp for garnish)

3 tbsp white wine

2 tbsp sherry

4 fl oz/100 ml fish stock

2 oz/50 g peas (fresh or frozen), cooked

2 tsp mixed tarragon, dill, parsley

juice of ½ lemon

salt & freshly ground pepper

METHOD

Heat oil in a non-stick pan. Add shallots or onion, garlic and chilli and sweat until transparent but without colouring. Add prawns and sweat for a further minute. Season, remove from pan and keep aside.

SAUCE

Heat the oil in a large saucepan, add the peppers and sweat for a minute. Add the tomatoes and sweat for a minute. Add white wine and sherry and bring to the boil. Add fish stock and simmer for 15 minutes. Season and add the reserved tomatoes.

TO FINISH OFF

Mix prawns with sauce and bring to the boil. Add peas, herbs and lemon juice and, if necessary, adjust the seasoning to taste.

Garnish with coriander leaves if desired.

SHELLING PRAWNS

The easiest way to shell a cooked prawn is to hold it between two fingers. Gently pull off the tail shell and twist off the head. Then you can peel away its soft body shell, along with the small crawler claws.

BREAKFAST

Most of us underestimate the importance of breakfast. There is no better way to start the day than to have a good, balanced meal full of vitamins, fibre and protein.

Unfortunately, too few of us give ourselves this treat each day. We tend to forget that, during the night, our bodies have been without nourishment for about 8 hours, so a hearty, but healthy breakfast is a sound idea.

Different cultures have different habits and tastes. But one factor that I cannot ignore, as the Executive Chef of one of the great hotels of the world, is the trend towards healthier eating.

For this reason we have introduced The Dorchester Breakfast "Leger" - fresh orange or grapefruit juice to start, followed by traditional Bircher muesli with low-fat yoghurt, fresh fruits and berries and an egg white omelette with herbs or mushrooms and low-fat cottage cheese.

This is served with a basket of wholemeal rolls, brown toast and pumpkin muffins, all baked early in the morning in our bakery and served with marmalade and soya margarine.

I can assure you, this will give anyone a boost to a successful day.

Bran Muffins with Sesame Seeds (top) & Bircher Muesli (below)

Bircher Muesli

Serves 6

CALORIES
Approximately 240 per portion

INGREDIENTS
3 oz/75 g oats
1 oz/25 g sultanas
8 fl oz/250 ml low fat yoghurt, plain or fruit
5 oz/150 g low-fat cottage cheese
½ pt/300 ml low-fat milk
1 orange, peeled and segmented
1 apple, grated
1 banana, peeled and sliced
2 oz/50 g sugar
10 oz/250 g fruit/berries as desired
1 tbsp toasted hazelnuts, chopped
1 tbsp walnuts, chopped

METHOD

The night before eating, mix together the oats, sultanas, yoghurt, cottage cheese and milk in a bowl to allow the oats to absorb the liquid. Cover and refrigerate.

Just before eating, add the orange segments, apple and banana slices. Add the sugar, followed by the soft fruits, hazelnuts and walnuts.

NOTE

If you prefer, replace the sugar with a sweetener. Also, this basic recipe can be altered to your own taste by adding different berries or dried fruits. If you do not fancy cottage cheese, just leave it out and add a few more oats.

Bran Muffins with Sesame Seeds

Makes about 40 muffins

CALORIES
Approximately 210 per muffin

INGREDIENTS
2 eggs
13 oz/375 g soft brown sugar
5 fl oz/150 ml sunflower oil
18 fl oz/500 ml skimmed milk
1 tsp vanilla essence
4 oz/100 g bran
2 tsp bicarbonate of soda
15 oz/425 g granary flour
½ tsp salt
7 oz/200 g sultanas or dates
sesame seeds

OVEN TEMPERATURE
180°C/350°F/Gas Mark 4

METHOD

Beat the eggs and sugar well. Add the oil, milk, vanilla and remaining ingredients and mix to a wet dough.

To bake, fill the muffin tins two-thirds full. Sprinkle with sesame seeds and bake for about 25-30 minutes until cooked.

CONVENIENCE MUFFINS

Make up the muffin mixture at your convenience and keep it in a closed container in the refrigerator for up to 4 days.
You'll find that the mixture will thicken with keeping. Just thin it down by adding a few tablespoons of water before use.

PANCAKES

Pancakes are incredibly versatile; eat them plain or filled, serve them savoury or sweet, as a starter, a light meal or for dessert. Whichever way you choose, they're sure to be enjoyed by everyone.

When you have made your mixture, it will keep for up to 2 days, covered, in the refrigerator. It might thicken slightly, so add a little milk to thin it down. But it is really better to fry the pancakes straight away, remove from the pan and leave them to cool on a rack. Do not lay them on top of each other while still warm, or they will stick together.

To store them, put greaseproof paper between each pancake, stack them and wrap the whole pile in clingfilm or tin foil and store in the refrigerator for 2-3 days.

For a light meal try them with stir-fried vegetables, strips of chicken and soya sauce, minced meat or vegetable curry accompanied by natural yoghurt with coriander. Or fry or grill a slice of ham, place it on top of the pancake with three pieces of cooked green asparagus, then roll into a cigar shape and serve with wild mushroom or tomato sauce, or add plum sauce for an Oriental touch.

But remember that pancakes are also ideal as a sweet treat. Follow the same basic recipe, but add some sugar to your taste or some vanilla essence. Also, there is no limit to the fillings - just experiment!

Pancakes with Olives and Pesto Sauce (left) & Onion, Mushroom and Bacon Pancakes (right)

Basic Pancake Recipe

Makes 12-14 pancakes (6 in/15 cm in diameter) with approximately 85 calories each

INGREDIENTS
vegetable oil for cooking
4 oz/100 g flour
8 fl oz/250 ml milk
1 oz/25 g butter, melted
3 eggs, lightly whisked
salt & freshly ground pepper
nutmeg

METHOD
Mix together milk, flour and butter into a smooth batter. Add the eggs. Season.
Heat a non-stick pan, grease with oil, pour in the mixture (not too thick) and brown the pancake equally on each side.
Remove from the pan and place on a cooling rack.
Keep aside until ready for use.

Pancakes with Olives and Pesto Sauce

Serves 4 (2 pancakes each)

CALORIES
Approximately 410 calories per portion

INGREDIENTS: PANCAKES
Follow basic recipe as above

FILLING
1 tbsp olive oil
1 shallot or ¼ onion, peeled and finely chopped
½ clove garlic, peeled and crushed
3 medium tomatoes, peeled, seeded and coarsely chopped
1 green pepper, chopped
1 yellow pepper, chopped
12 stuffed olives, cut into fine rings
2 anchovy fillets, finely chopped
salt & freshly ground pepper

PESTO SAUCE
1 tbsp pine kernels
1½ tbsp parsley, finely chopped
1½ tsp basil, finely chopped
½ clove garlic, peeled and crushed
2½ tbsp olive oil
4 tbsp double cream
salt & freshly ground pepper

OVEN TEMPERATURE
200°C/400°F/Gas Mark 6

METHOD
Pancakes: Make 8 following the basic recipe provided above.

FILLING
Heat the olive oil and sweat the shallot or onion and the garlic until transparent, but without colouring. Add the tomatoes and cook for 2-3 minutes. Add the peppers and cook until tender. Add the olive rings and anchovies. Season.

The final mixture should be fairly dry with hardly any moisture left. If there appears to be too much liquid remaining, boil the mixture until the excess has evaporated. Keep aside.

PESTO SAUCE
Roast the pine kernels under the grill until golden. Cool, then chop very finely. Add the herbs and garlic and season. Stir in the olive oil and cream.

TO FINISH OFF
Divide the filling into equal portions.

Place the pancakes in front of you and arrange the filling in the centre across the pancakes. Fold one side of each pancake over to make a half moon shape.

Heat in the oven for about 2-3 minutes. Remove and pour over the pesto sauce.

FREEZING PANCAKES

For an excellent standby, double or treble the basic pancake recipe, cook and wrap pancakes, then freeze them. To thaw, leave at room temperature for 2-3 hours. You can also reheat, after removing wrappings, in a warm oven for 5 minutes, or on a plate over boiling water for about 10 minutes.

Onion, Mushroom and Bacon Pancakes

Serves 4

CALORIES
Approximately 440 per portion

INGREDIENTS:PANCAKES
Make 4 pancakes from Basic Pancake Recipe
on page 31 and set aside

FILLING
3 rashers streaky bacon, cut into strips
7 oz/200 g button mushrooms, sliced
24 silverskin onions, fresh or in brine
2 medium tomatoes, peeled, seeds removed

SAUCE
1 tbsp vegetable oil
1 shallot or ¼ onion, peeled and chopped
½ clove garlic, peeled and crushed
4 fl oz/100 ml red wine
7 fl oz/200 ml chicken or beef stock
1 tsp cornflour
1 tsp fresh parsley, chopped
salt & freshly ground pepper

OVEN TEMPERATURE
200°C/400°F/Gas Mark 6

METHOD:

SAUCE

Heat the oil and sweat shallots or onion with the garlic until transparent, but without colouring. Add the wine, bring to the boil and cook until half the quantity remains. Add the stock, bring to the boil and continue to boil over medium heat for 2-3 minutes.

Dissolve the cornflour in 2 tbsp cold water, add to the sauce and boil for 2 minutes. Season, pass the mixture through a sieve and keep aside.

FILLING

Heat a non-stick pan and fry the bacon strips until crisp. Remove and keep aside. Reheat the fat remaining in the pan, add the mushrooms and fry for about 1 minute until cooked. Remove from the pan and keep aside.

Reheat the same pan, add the silverskin onions and brown slightly. Chop the tomatoes into ¼ in (½ cm) cubes, add to the pan and cook for 2 minutes. Add the mushrooms and the bacon strips. Season and add the parsley.

TO FINISH OFF

Fill the pancakes as described in Pancakes with Olives and Pesto Sauce on page 31, place in an ovenproof dish and heat for 2 minutes. Bring the sauce to the boil, add the parsley and pour over the pancakes.

Pancakes with Cream Cheese and Black Cherries

Serves 4

CALORIES
Approximately 280 per portion

INGREDIENTS: PANCAKES
Make 8 pancakes from Basic Pancake Recipe
on page 31 and keep aside.

FILLING
8 tbsp cream cheese
4 tsp icing sugar
1 lb/450 g tinned, stoneless black cherries,
drained (save liquid for sauce)
1 tsp grated orange peel

SAUCE
liquid from cherries
juice of 2 oranges
2 tbsp cornflour
brandy to taste

OVEN TEMPERATURE
180° C/350°F/Gas Mark 4

METHOD

Mix the cream cheese with the cherries and icing sugar. Add the orange peel to the mixture. Spread the mixture evenly over the 8 pancakes about ¼ in/½ cm thick. Roll the pancakes into a sausage shape and place in an oven-proof dish. Heat in the oven for about 10 minutes. In the meantime prepare the sauce.

SAUCE

Pour the liquid from the cherries into a saucepan and add the orange juice. Bring to the boil. Dissolve the cornflour in 2 tbsp water and add to the boiling liquid. Simmer for a few minutes.

TO FINISH OFF

Remove the pancakes from the oven. Reheat the sauce, add brandy to taste and pour over the pancakes. Serve.

VEGETARIAN

Many of us enjoy meals without meat - in fact more and more people are turning to vegetarian dishes. Some do so for health reasons. Others because it offers a less expensive alternative, whilst providing good nourishment. Others simply because they enjoy the delicious combinations of flavours on offer.

Whatever the reason, with vegetable produce imported from all over the world, there is no denying that, in preparing a vegetarian dish, we are spoilt for choice with the endless array of ingredients on offer.

Vegetarian cooking offers an exciting opportunity to experiment with new flavours, new textures and novel combinations of ingredients. And not only do the dishes taste delicious, they also offer excellent nutrition, are low in fat and high in fibre.

Of course, if you are planning to cut out all meat products from your diet, make sure that you replace them with alternative sources of protein - pulses, beans, nuts, cheese or eggs - which are essential for good health.

Vegetables lend themselves well to a host of cooking styles, from the simplest of home cooking to the most exotic of dishes. Most of us enjoy something different, so why not tempt your family with a meatless meal?

Baked Vegetable and Rice Omelette

Serves 4

CALORIES
Approximately 230 per portion

INGREDIENTS
3 tbsp long grain rice
4 oz/100 g green beans, cut into ½ in/1 cm strips
2 oz/50 g peas
6 eggs, size 3
2 tbsp vegetable oil
1 red pepper, cut in half and sliced into strips ⅛ in/3 mm thick
½ onion, peeled and finely sliced
1 clove garlic, peeled and crushed
12 olives, black or green, cut in half
1 tomato, medium size, peeled, deseeded and coarsely chopped
salt & freshly ground pepper
1 tsp soya sauce
1 tsp parsley and coriander, finely chopped

OVEN TEMPERATURE
190°C/375°F/Gas Mark 5

METHOD
Cook the rice in salted water. Refresh in cold running water. Drain and keep aside. Cook the green beans in salted water. Refresh in cold water. Drain and keep aside. Cook the peas in salted water. Refresh in cold water, drain and keep aside.

Beat the eggs lightly.

TO FINISH OFF
Heat the oil in a large, non-stick, oven-proof pan. Add the peppers, onion and garlic and sweat for about 3 minutes without colouring. Add the bean pieces and olives. Add the cooked rice, tomato and peas.

Season with salt, pepper and soya sauce. Add the parsley and coriander. Pour the egg mixture over and stir.

Cook in the oven for about 20 minutes until golden brown.

Remove from the oven and place on a warm serving dish. Garnish to taste and serve.

Vegetable Pie

Serves 4

CALORIES
Approximately 370 per portion

INGREDIENTS
flour to dust pastry
½ lb/225 g puff pastry (made with vegetable margarine)
1 egg for egg wash

SAUCE
1 tbsp vegetable oil
½ onion, peeled and finely chopped
1 clove garlic, peeled and crushed
1 red pepper, chopped
½ pt/300 ml vegetable stock
salt & freshly ground pepper

PIE FILLING
1 potato, medium size
1 small cauliflower
4 oz/100 g peas
2 tbsp vegetable oil
½ onion, peeled and sliced
1 clove garlic, peeled and crushed
1 yellow pepper cut into thumb sized pieces
2 courgettes, medium size, cut into ½ in/1 cm rings

OVEN TEMPERATURE
190°C/375°F/Gas Mark 5

METHOD

Roll out the puff pastry about ⅛ in/3 mm thick until it is large enough to cover a pie dish. Rest in the refrigerator for 20 minutes.

SAUCE

Heat the oil in a saucepan. Add the onion and garlic and sweat for 1 minute without colouring. Add the red pepper and sweat for a minute.

Add the vegetable stock, cover with a lid and cook on medium heat until the pepper is cooked. Puree in a food blender.

Place back in a pan, bring to the boil and season with salt and pepper. Remove from the heat and keep aside.

FILLING

Cook the potato in its skin. Remove the skin, leave to cool and cut into ½ in/1 cm pieces. Keep aside.

Divide the cauliflower into florets. Cook in salted water. Refresh in cold water and drain. Cook the peas in salted water, refresh in cold water and drain.

Heat the oil in a large saucepan. Add the onion and garlic and sweat until transparent but without colouring. Add the yellow pepper and sweat for a further minute.

Add the red pepper sauce and cook until the yellow pepper is cooked but still crisp. Add the courgette rings and boil for 1 minute, then add the cauliflower, peas and potatoes. Season with salt and pepper. Remove from the heat and leave to cool.

TO FINISH OFF

Spoon the vegetable mixture into a pie dish and make sure there is a space of 1 in/2.5 cm space between the filling and the top of the dish.

Brush the border of the dish with egg wash or milk. Cut a strip of puff pastry ½ in/1 cm wide and press on top of the border all around the dish.

Brush again with egg wash or milk. Cut the puff pastry to the size of the pie dish and cover the dish with it. Brush with egg wash or milk. Bake in the oven for about 30-40 minutes until golden brown.

Serve immediately.

VEGETABLE STOCK

Vegetable stock is essential in vegetarian cooking. To make a tasty stock, take a variety of non-starchy (e.g. not potato) vegetables, wash and place in a pan. Add a bay leaf, a bouquet of mixed herbs and peppercorns, then cover with cold water. Bring to the boil slowly, then reduce the heat and allow to simmer gently for about 1 hour. Strain, then reduce. Cool and freeze in small quantities until required.

Vegetable Pie (top) & Baked Vegetable and Rice Omelette (below)

TROUT

Trout, once thought of in terms of pure luxury, is now widely available at reasonable prices, thanks to the introduction of fish farming. Generally speaking, trout falls into three categories. The most commonly available is rainbow trout, which is bred in specially-conditioned tanks on fish farms. Green-gold in colour with white, delicate flesh, this type weighs from 6-10 oz (150 g-250 g) and is available all year round, both fresh and frozen.

Less widely available, but considered superior to the rainbow trout, is the river or brown trout. This has darker, spotted skin and its flesh colour varies according to habitat and feeding. The river trout is available from March to September.

Finally, there is the sea or salmon trout. This is similar to salmon with silvery scales and firm, pink flesh. These fish are usually sold whole and weigh 2-6 lb (900 g-2.7 kg).

Sea or salmon trout is best cooked like salmon, whilst the river or brown trout can be grilled or fried for the best flavour. Rainbow trout, on the other hand, lends itself not only to grilling, but also to poaching and baking. Rainbow trout can be used in many recipes. Popular methods of preparation include pan-frying with almonds or with capers and lemon juice, or simply poached with white wine or fish stock as a healthy alternative. Or serve it in a white sauce with a flavouring of your choice, such as herbs or tomato.

Trout is also delicious smoked. In this case, no cooking is required and it can be served simply with a salad and horse-radish-flavoured mayonnaise. Or remove the fine bones, then flake the flesh, add strips of radish and cucumber, mix with a light salad dressing and herbs and serve with boiled new potatoes.

Trout with Orange and Tarragon Sauce

Serves 4

CALORIES
Approximately 370 per portion

INGREDIENTS
8 trout fillets
1 tbsp butter
1 shallot or ¼ onion, peeled and finely chopped
7 fl oz/200 ml white wine
1 orange, peeled and segmented
salt & freshly ground pepper

SAUCE
½ tbsp butter at room temperature
½ tbsp flour
cooking liquid from above
2 fl oz/50 ml fish stock
7 fl oz/200 ml single cream
1 tsp tarragon, finely chopped
1 tsp parsley, finely chopped
salt & freshly ground pepper

OVEN TEMPERATURE
180°C/350°F/Gas Mark 4

METHOD
Brush an oven-proof dish or tray with butter and place trout fillets in it next to each other, skin side up. Season and keep aside.

Put the shallot or onion in a saucepan, add the white wine, bring to the boil and simmer for 1 minute. Pass through a sieve, pour over the fish and arrange the orange segments on top.

Cook in the oven for about 5 minutes. Remove from the oven. Remove the orange segments from the top of the fish and place on a serving dish. Remove the skin from the fish. This is best done using a knife to lift the skin from the thick part of the fish and pulling it carefully towards the small tail end. Using a spatula, very carefully transfer the trout fillets onto the orange segments. Keep warm. Reserve the cooking liquid.

SAUCE
Whisk together the butter and flour into a smooth paste and keep aside.

Place cooking liquid from above into a saucepan and bring to the boil. Add fish stock and boil again. Add cream and boil.

Add the butter and flour mixture and boil for 3 minutes. Season, remove from heat and add the tarragon and parsley.

Pour over the trout fillets and serve.

Trout with Orange and Tarragon Sauce

Smoked Trout and Avocado Soup

Serves 4

CALORIES
Approximately 385 calories per portion

INGREDIENTS
2 tbsp vegetable oil
1 shallot or ¼ onion, peeled and finely chopped
3 smoked trout fillets - discard all tiny bones
half a ripe avocado, peeled, stoned and coarsely chopped
juice of 1 lemon
7 fl oz/200 ml white wine
1 pt/600 ml fish stock
7 fl oz/200 ml milk
salt & freshly ground pepper
1 tbsp grated horseradish
1 tsp dill

METHOD
Heat the oil in a saucepan. Sweat the shallot or onion until transparent but without colouring. Add the trout fillets and sweat for 1 minute. Add the avocado flesh and stir. Add the lemon juice and white wine and bring to the boil. Add the fish stock and bring back to the boil. Simmer for 10 minutes. Add the milk and simmer for a further 5 minutes. Liquidise.

TO FINISH OFF
Bring back to the boil. Add the horseradish and season. Add the dill and serve.

COOKING WHOLE TROUT

When cooking trout whole, leave the head on. The eyes will turn white when the flesh is cooked to perfection. To pan-fry a whole trout, make three small incisions on each side, and fry in some vegetable oil with a whole clove of garlic and a sprig of rosemary. Baste the fish often to allow the flavour to penetrate the flesh.

HAM

Ham is often associated with special occasions, particularly Christmas, but it can, of course, be enjoyed in many variations at any time of year.

Strictly speaking, ham comes from the hind leg of the pig and is removed from the carcass before salting and curing according to local recipes. It differs in this respect from gammon, which is cut from the carcass after brining. Shoulder and collar cuts of bacon are also cured in a similar way to ham, although their flavour is somewhat more robust. All, however, are similar enough to interchange in recipes without adversely affecting the end result.

A whole ham will weigh between 10-16 lb (4.5-7.2 kg), and may be bought whole or, more often, sliced. When buying a whole ham, choose one that is short, thick and not too fatty. Cooked slices should look fresh with pink flesh and white fat.

More often than not hams are cooked prior to purchase. If not, follow instructions carefully, as cooking will depend on the type of curing. Soaking will also be necessary and will vary from 12-24 hours.

Amongst the best known English cooking hams are Bradenham, Suffolk, Wiltshire and York. Bradenham Ham is small and not easy to obtain. It is soaked in molasses rather than salt, resulting in a black rind, reddish meat and a delicate, sweet flavour. Suffolk Ham is cured in a similar way, resulting in a full, delicate flavour. Wiltshire Ham is really gammon, since it is cured before being cut from the carcass. As it is mild cured, it does not keep as well. It is the least expensive type of ham. York Ham is probably the best known of all and is most popular at Christmas. It is dry-cured and lightly smoked with a tender, mild flavour.

Ham is most often eaten cold, but is delicious eaten warm topped with a glaze. It can be used in a variety of ways, such as with salad, mixed with pasta, or added to pea or lentil soup. Try slices of cooked ham rolled and filled with cooked ratatouille and baked in the oven. A slice of ham on toast topped with slices of pineapple or tomato covered with cheese and browned under the grill makes a tasty snack.

Baked Layers of Ham with Aubergines and Tomatoes (left) & Ham Rolls Filled with Dried Apricots (right)

Baked Layers of Ham with Aubergines and Tomatoes

Serves 2

CALORIES
Approximately 570 per portion

INGREDIENTS
2 tbsp vegetable oil

1 aubergine cut into ⅛ in/3 mm rings
flour to dust aubergine rings
6 slices ham
2 medium-sized tomatoes, peeled and cut into ⅛ in/3 mm rings
1 tsp basil, finely chopped

CHEESE SAUCE
3 tbsp vegetable oil
1½ oz/40 g flour
10 fl oz/300 ml milk
7 fl oz/200 ml vegetable stock
salt & freshly ground pepper
nutmeg
3 tbsp grated Parmesan or Cheddar cheese

OVEN TEMPERATURE
200°C/400°F/Gas mark 6

METHOD
Heat the oil in a non-stick pan. Season the aubergine rings with salt and freshly ground pepper, and dust with flour. Fry the rings in the oil until golden brown on each side. Remove from the pan and keep aside.

SAUCE
Warm the oil in a saucepan. Add the flour and mix. Add the cold milk and bring to the boil (it will be thick). Add the cold vegetable stock, and bring to the boil, stirring constantly with a whisk. Season with salt, pepper and nutmeg. Simmer for about 10 minutes. Pass through a sieve. Add 1 tbsp of grated cheese.

TO FINISH OFF
Place 2 slices of ham in an oven-proof dish. Place one slice of tomato and one slice of aubergine on top. Season with freshly ground pepper. Sprinkle a little basil on top. Place the next layer of ham on top, and again add a layer of tomato and aubergine. Cover with a third layer of ham. Pour the cheese sauce over the ham, making sure that it is completely covered. Sprinkle the cheese on top. Bake in the oven for about 20 minutes and serve hot.

Ham Rolls Filled with Dried Apricots

Serves 4

CALORIES
Approximately 270 per portion

INGREDIENTS
4 dried apricots, finely chopped
8 slices cooked ham

FILLING
1 tbsp vegetable oil
1 tbsp flour
7 fl oz/200 ml milk
5 fl oz/150 ml chicken stock
3 tsp gelatine powder
9 oz/250 g cooked ham, fat removed and cut into small cubes
1 tsp brandy
1 tbsp port wine
4 fl oz/100 ml whipped cream
salt and freshly ground pepper
1 tbsp parsley, finely chopped

GARNISH
salad leaves

METHOD
Keep the finely chopped apricots and slices of ham to one side.

FILLING
Heat the oil. Remove the pan from the heat and stir in the flour. Add the milk, stir and bring to the boil. Simmer on low heat for 2 minutes. Cool and keep aside. Heat the chicken stock. Remove from heat and sprinkle over gelatine powder. Add to white sauce. Add the cubes of ham to the mixture. Place the bowl over ice. Stir the mixture thoroughly. Add the brandy and port wine. When the mixture starts to thicken, fold in the whipped cream. Add the dried apricots and parsley. Season.

TO FINISH OFF
Divide the mixture equally and spread evenly on top of the slices of ham. Carefully roll up each slice of ham and leave to set in the refrigerator. Arrange on plates or a serving dish and garnish with some salad leaves. Serve as a starter or light meal.

PINEAPPLE

There are many different varieties of pineapple and they vary enormously in size and colour. Pick a good one, and the flavour is quite delicious. The sweet, firm, yellowy-cream flesh is hidden by hard, knobbly top skin, which varies from yellow-green to orange-brown. No matter what the size or colour, when buying, choose one with firm, green leaves.

The hard exterior often makes it difficult to determine when the fruit has reached optimum ripeness - nothing is more disappointing than anticipating the sweet, juicy flesh, only to discover that the pineapple is underripe and tart, or overripe and browning. The trick to this is to test the leaves: grasp a central leaf and pull gently - if it comes out easily, the fruit is ripe.

Pineapple is often available freshly sliced or tinned in juice or sugar syrup, as well as whole.

It makes a delicious dessert served "au naturel" sliced or cubed, or with cheese, cottage cheese or fromage frais. Alternatively, marinate slices in a little liqueur for about 2 hours before serving.

Of course pineapple also lends itself to savoury dishes. Try it in salads with chicken or ham, or diced with cashew nuts and rice. Serve it warm as fritters to garnish a curry, grilled with gammon rashers or, for a quick snack, sliced on toast, smothered with melted cheese.

Pork Stew with Pineapple and Peppers

Serves 4

CALORIES
Approximately 520 per portion

INGREDIENTS
1 tbsp vegetable oil
2 shallots or 1 small onion, peeled and finely chopped
1 green pepper, chopped
1 red pepper, chopped
2 tbsp tomato ketchup
1½ lb/675 g pork (shoulder or neck), no bones and cut into cubes
3 tbsp flour for dusting meat cubes
3 tbsp vegetable oil
6 rings tinned pineapple, drained and quartered (reserve 3 tbsp juice for sauce)

SAUCE
6 tbsp pineapple juice from above
2 fl oz/50 ml white wine
1¼ pt/750 ml chicken stock
4 fl oz/100 ml single cream
1 tbsp cornflour
4 tbsp water (to dissolve cornflour)
salt & freshly ground pepper

GARNISH
1 tsp fresh coriander leaves, finely chopped

OVEN TEMPERATURE
180°C/350°F/Gas Mark 4

METHOD
Heat the oil very gently in an oven-proof dish. Sweat the shallots or onion until transparent but without colouring. Add the peppers and sweat for a further 2 minutes then remove from heat. Add tomato ketchup and keep aside.

Dust pork cubes with flour. Heat remaining oil in a non-stick pan and add cubes of pork. Brown on all sides and season with salt and pepper. (Do not brown all the pieces at the same time. Divide meat into three portions so that there is enough space in the pan for all the meat to brown thoroughly).

Remove meat from pan and place on top of shallot and pepper mixture in the oven-proof dish. Add pineapple juice and white wine. Bring to the boil and add stock. Bring back to the boil, cover with a lid and bake in the oven for about 1¼ hours or until meat is cooked. Add pineapple pieces and simmer for a further 2 minutes.

To FINISH OFF
Remove the meat from the cooking dish using a perforated spoon and place in a serving dish. Bring cooking liquid to the boil. Add cream and bring back to the boil. Add dissolved cornflour, boil for 2-3 minutes and season.

Pour the sauce over the meat and sprinkle with coriander leaves before serving.

PINEAPPLE PARTY PIECE

For an exotic party piece, halve a pineapple lengthwise, including the leaves. Remove the flesh without cutting the skin. Remove the woody centre part if necessary. Cut the flesh into cubes and put back into the pineapple shell. Sprinkle with pistachio nuts, raisins or roasted pine kernels. Used in this way, pineapple shells also make attractive "containers" for fruit salads, sorbets or ice-cream.

Pineapple and Coconut Cream with Raspberry Sauce (top) & Pork Stew with Pineapple and Peppers (below)

Pineapple and Coconut Cream with Raspberry Sauce

Serves 4

CALORIES
Approximately 325 per portion

INGREDIENTS
1 lb/450 g tinned pineapple rings, drained (reserve liquid)
2 tbsp cornflour
2 tbsp desiccated coconut
pinch ginger
4 oz/100 g cream cheese
4 fl oz/100 ml whipping cream

SAUCE
9 oz/250 g raspberries (fresh or frozen)
2 oz/50 g icing sugar
2 tbsp water
juice of 1 orange

GARNISH
1 pineapple ring cut into 4 pieces
4 raspberries
fresh mint

METHOD
Mix 4 tbsp pineapple liquid with the cornflour. Keep aside. Reserve 1 ring of pineapple and cut the remainder into small pieces. Keep aside.

Bring remaining pineapple liquid to the boil. Add ginger and desiccated coconut. Simmer for 1 minute. Add dissolved cornflour and bring back to the boil, stirring constantly. Add pineapple pieces. Remove from heat and leave to cool. Add cream cheese and mix thoroughly with a spatula. Whip cream and fold into the mixture. Spoon or pipe into individual glass bowls or ramekins and keep in the refrigerator for at least 3 hours before serving.

SAUCE
Place raspberries in a saucepan and add icing sugar. Add water and orange juice. Bring to the boil. Liquidise, pass through a sieve and leave to cool.

TO FINISH OFF
Take cream from the fridge and garnish with a pineapple wedge, raspberry and a sprig of mint. Serve sauce separately.

AVOCADO PEARS

Once a luxury that had to be imported from countries enjoying a sub-tropical climate, today avocados can be bought and enjoyed at any time of year.

Although correctly classified as a fruit, avocados are usually eaten as a savoury, rather than as a dessert. However, in some tropical countries where they grow, they are also used in sweet dishes.

There is a big difference between the composition of an avocado and that of other fruit. An avocado contains approximately 70% water and 30% poly-unsaturated oil. It is also rich in goodness, containing about 11 different vitamins and various minerals, such as calcium and iron.

Avocados are usually shaped like pears, but can vary considerably in size, from that of a modest dessert pear to the generous proportions of a large papaya. The skin colour differs too, ranging from deep purple to green, but the flesh is always pale green, oily and soft with the consistency of butter.

To use avocados, cut them in half with a stainless steel knife, remove the stone and peel if necessary. As the flesh discolours quickly, always prepare them at the last minute or rub the cut surface with lemon juice or vinegar to prevent discolouration. Ripe pears can be frozen. Peel and mash allowing 1 tbsp lemon juice to each avocado.

Unpeeled avocado halves are usually filled with vinaigrette or prawns. For something a little different, simply mash the flesh with a fork, season to taste and spread on a slice of bread, or make a tasty sandwich of avocado with smoked salmon or tuna fish or mixed with some Stilton cheese. Alternatively, peel and use sliced or cubed: their smooth creamy texture and flavour will add interest to any salad. Toss the cubes gently with tuna and potato in a spicy dressing or try them with chicken and bacon.

Their smooth texture is also ideally suited to dips - Mexican Guacamole is a popular favourite served with crudités, corn chips or pitta bread. Or serve Guacamole and soured cream with your next Chilli Con Carne - the flavours complement each other deliciously.

For a tropical treat, serve an avocado cream dessert: scoop out the flesh, liquidise with the juice of a lemon or lime, add 4 fl oz (100 ml) whipped cream and some icing sugar. Finally add a dash of sherry and served chilled in glasses with sponge fingers. Or try avocado in a fruit salad, diced with passion fruit and raspberries.

Chilled Curried Avocado and Apple Soup

Serves 6

CALORIES
Approximately 235 per portion

INGREDIENTS
1 Golden Delicious apple, peeled and seeds removed
2 medium-sized ripe avocados, peeled, stones removed
1 tbsp curry powder
juice of 1 lemon
1¼ pts/750 ml vegetable stock, chilled
8 fl oz/250 ml fromage frais
salt & freshly ground pepper

GARNISH
2 tbsp toasted flaked almonds

METHOD
Cut an apple quarter into fine cubes, squeeze a little lemon juice over to avoid discolouring and keep aside as a garnish.

Place the remaining apple, avocado, curry powder, lemon juice and stock in a blender and puree.

TO FINISH OFF
Add the fromage frais, blend again and season with salt and pepper.

Pour into a bowl, add the diced apples, sprinkle with toasted almonds and serve.

RIPENING AVOCADOS
As they are imported, avocados are usually unripe when purchased.
For this reason, always buy avocados at least 3 days in advance of using and allow them to ripen at room temperature. To test, gently press the large rounded end which will yield slightly when the avocado is ready for eating.

Poached Chicken Breasts with Avocado and Watercress Sauce

Serves 4

CALORIES
Approximately 380 per portion

INGREDIENTS
¾ pt/450 ml chicken stock

4 chicken breasts, skin removed

SAUCE
2 tbsp vegetable oil

1 shallot or ¼ onion, peeled and chopped

1 medium-sized, ripe avocado pear, peeled with stone removed

juice of 1 lemon

1 small bunch watercress, leaves only

salt & freshly ground pepper

METHOD
Bring the chicken stock to the boil. Add the chicken breasts. Reduce heat, cover and simmer for 8 minutes. Remove and keep warm. Reserve stock for the sauce.

SAUCE
Heat the oil in a saucepan. Sweat the shallot or onion until transparent but without colouring. Cut the avocado into thumb-sized cubes and add to the pan with the lemon juice. Bring to the boil. Add the hot stock and simmer for 5 minutes. Add the watercress leaves, bring to the boil and season. Puree the sauce in a blender and pass through a sieve.

TO FINISH OFF
Bring back to the boil.
Place the chicken breasts in a serving dish and pour the sauce over.

ASPARAGUS

Although imported asparagus is on sale in the shops from early spring onwards, English asparagus is only available between May and June. These spears are slightly more expensive, but the flavour is quite delicious. Asparagus is also extremely low in calories, high in fibre and a good source of Vitamin A, so it's well worth treating yourself when it's in season.

Asparagus can be bought loose or in bundles and is graded according to the plumpness of the stem and tip. These factors, of course, affect the price, so, when buying, consider what you intend to do with the asparagus: whether you are going to eat it whole, in a salad or in a soup. Always ensure that it is fresh. Look for small to medium-sized spears with tight, well-formed purple or green tips, and avoid those that are large with dry, woody stems.

To prepare, remove the bottom of the stems: hold the spear in both hands near the base and gently 'snap' the end off - it will break cleanly where the tender flesh joins the woody stem - or use a knife and cut approximately one inch off the end. If the spears are very large, the stems may need to be scraped or peeled towards the base.

Traditionally, asparagus is then tied in bundles - enough for one person - and cooked upright, dropped into plenty of boiling, salted water.

An alternative method, which avoids the necessity of bundling, is suitable for small amounts: lie the spears - all facing in the same direction - in a frying pan of boiling, salted water. Then position the pan over the heat, so that only the water over the stems boils - not that over the tips. Either method will require about 12-15 minutes cooking time for medium-sized spears, so that the stems are cooked through whilst the tips are not over-cooked. I prefer to eat asparagus slightly crisp. Remove a spear from the pan occasionally and bite to test whether it is tender.

If you want to serve the asparagus spears cold, have a large bowl of iced water standing by, and, when they are cooked to your taste, plunge them into the iced water immediately. This stops them cooking and sets the brilliant green colour. When required, drain well on a kitchen towel and serve with melted butter, vinaigrette or mustard-flavoured mayonnaise.

If you want to be more adventurous, try asparagus warm with an orange-flavoured Hollandaise sauce.

Whichever way you choose, make the most of your purchase by saving the trimmings and cooking water for soups, sauces and dressings.

Asparagus Salad

Serves 4

CALORIES
Approximately 140 per portion

INGREDIENTS
1¾ pts/1 ltr water (to cook asparagus)
20 asparagus spears
4 oz/100 g mixed salad leaves, washed
½ oz/15 g walnuts, chopped
fresh chervil for garnish

DRESSING
1 tsp coarse grain mustard
4 tsp red wine vinegar
2 fl oz/50 ml sunflower oil
1 tsp walnut oil
2 tsp asparagus stock
½ tsp fresh chervil, chopped
salt & freshly ground white pepper

METHOD:

SALAD
Prepare the asparagus and remove the ends (reserving the trimmings for soup). Cook in boiling, salted water. (Reserve stock for salad dressing and soup). Cut off tips about 3 inches (7.5 cm) from top. Keep to one side.

Cut the stems into pieces - about 1 inch (2.5 cm) in length.

DRESSING
In a large bowl mix all the dressing ingredients thoroughly together and season.

TO FINISH OFF
Add the salad leaves and sliced asparagus stems to the dressing. Mix gently. Place on 4 serving plates, keeping to one half of the plate. Mix the tips in the dressing and dress on the opposite side of the plate.

Sprinkle some chopped walnuts over the salad and garnish with chervil.

Right: Asparagus Salad

Asparagus Soup

Serves 4

CALORIES
Approximately 250 per portion

INGREDIENTS
1 oz/25 g butter or vegetable oil
1 shallot, finely chopped
1 small clove of garlic, peeled and chopped
asparagus trimmings from previous recipe
1½ oz/40 g flour
1¼ pt/750 ml asparagus stock from previous recipe
7 fl oz/200 ml single cream
salt & freshly ground white pepper

GARNISH
4 spears of asparagus, cooked and cut into pieces about 1 inch (2.5 cm) long
½ tsp fresh chervil, chopped
½ tsp fresh chives, chopped

METHOD
Melt the butter in a saucepan and sweat the shallot and garlic on a medium heat until transparent. Add the asparagus trimmings and sweat for 1 minute.

Stir in the flour and cook for 2 minutes. Add one third of the cold asparagus stock. Stir and bring to the boil. Add the remaining stock and simmer for 30 minutes.

Liquidise in a blender and pass through a sieve into a saucepan. Bring to the boil. Add the cream and the cooked asparagus pieces. Season with salt and freshly ground white pepper.

TO FINISH OFF
Place the soup in bowls and sprinkle with chopped chives and chervil.

STORING ASPARAGUS

Asparagus is best eaten on the day of purchase. If storage is necessary, wrap the bundle in a damp cloth, ensuring that the tips are gently covered. Place in a plastic bag, seal and store upright in the fridge for not more than two days. Moisten the cloth each day.

RICE

Rice forms the staple diet of many countries. Here, however, we use it more often as an accompaniment to a main meal, often replacing our more popular starch, the potato. Its rather bland flavour combines extremely well with many others, making it an ideal accompaniment to other types of food and and a good basis for many dishes.

There are three main kinds of rice grain: long, medium and short. Long grains are fluffy and separate when cooked, making them ideal for using as an accompaniment or in risottos, salads and paellas. Medium grains are moister, making them ideal for dishes that need to bind together, such as stuffings, croquettes and moulds. Short grains are moist and sticky, making them ideal for sweet puddings.

Brown rice has increased in popularity over recent years. The grains are unpolished with only the inedible husk and bran removed, giving it a pleasant, nutty flavour. It can be treated in the same way as white rice, but will take longer to cook (about 30 minutes rather than 15) and will absorb more moisture.

Wild rice has particularly long grains. It is imported from America and, as the name implies, it originally grew wild. Although expensive, it is quite delicious and suitable for a special occasion, particularly with game.

During cooking, rice will approximately treble in bulk. When cooking it as an accompaniment, allow 2 oz/50 g per person; 1½ oz/40 g for a risotto or pilaff; and 1 oz/25 g for a salad. After cooking rice should be dry and slightly fluffy, not sticky or gluey.

Left-over boiled rice makes the ideal basis for a salad. Toss it in a well flavoured vinaigrette and serve cold with meat, fish or poultry. For a more substantial dish, add sultanas, spring onions, almonds and chopped ham or chicken.

Rice Hotpot

Serves 4
CALORIES
Approximately 660 per portion

INGREDIENTS
2 tbsp vegetable oil
4 chicken thighs

RICE
2 tbsp vegetable oil
2 tbsp shallot or onion, peeled and finely chopped
1 clove garlic, peeled and crushed
1 red pepper, deseeded and cut into cubes
1 green pepper, deseeded and cut into cubes
1 lb/450 g long grain rice
7 fl oz/200 ml dry white wine
1½ pt/900 ml chicken stock
salt & freshly ground white pepper
1 small stick cinnamon
¼ bay leaf
4 oz/100 g frozen peas
2 tomatoes, medium size, peeled, deseeded and cut into cubes
sprig of rosemary (optional)
olives (optional)

OVEN TEMPERATURE
180°C/350°F/Gas Mark 4

METHOD
Heat the vegetable oil in a non-stick pan. Season the chicken thighs and brown on both sides for about 5 minutes. Remove and keep aside.

RICE
Heat the vegetable oil in a deep oven-proof dish. Sweat the onion and garlic until transparent. Add the peppers and sweat for a minute. Add the rice and then sweat for a further minute.

Add the wine and bring to the boil. Add the chicken stock and bring back to the boil.

Add the chicken thighs and season. Add cinnamon stick and bay leaf. Cover with a lid and cook in the oven for 15 minutes.

Remove from the oven and add the frozen peas. Stir, replace the lid and return to the oven for another 6 minutes. Remove from the oven, add the tomato cubes and serve.

If you wish you can add some olives and rosemary.
A tomato, curry or pepper sauce would go well with this dish.

Garlic Prawns with Turmeric Risotto

Serves 2

CALORIES
Approximately 485 per portion

INGREDIENTS:

RISOTTO
1 tbsp vegetable oil
1 shallot or ¼ onion, peeled and finely chopped
1 clove garlic, peeled and crushed
4 oz/100 g risotto rice (Arborio, Camalino or pudding rice)
2 pinches turmeric
2 fl oz/50 ml dry white wine
10 fl oz/300 ml fish or vegetable stock
2 tbsp grated Parmesan cheese
½ oz/15 g butter

PRAWNS
2 tbsp vegetable oil
8 large prawns (if frozen, thaw before use)
½ clove garlic, peeled and crushed
1 tsp parsley, chopped
juice of half a lemon
salt & freshly ground pepper

GARNISH
your choice of herbs

METHOD:

RISOTTO

Heat the oil in a saucepan and add the shallots or onion and the garlic. Sweat until transparent, but without colouring.

Add the rice and turmeric and sweat for a further minute.

Add the wine and cook on a medium heat, stirring constantly.

Add some of the stock and stir frequently. Add the remainder of the stock and simmer until cooked (approximately 16 minutes).

Taste the risotto at this stage. If it needs to cook for longer, add a little more liquid until it is cooked to your taste.

Remove from the heat and add the Parmesan cheese. Season with salt and pepper.

Add the butter and keep warm.

PRAWNS

Heat the oil in a non-stick pan and add the seasoned prawns. Add the garlic and cook until golden brown.

Add the herbs and lemon juice.

TO FINISH OFF

Spoon the risotto onto plates and arrange the prawns on top.

Garnish with herbs.

COOKING PERFECT RICE
To ensure that you obtain tender, separate grains of rice, follow this method for boiling white rice. First rinse it under cold water until it is free of loose starch. Then, in a large pan, bring to the boil twice the quantity of water or stock for each measure of rice. Add the rice. As soon as the water boils again, cover with a tight lid and place on a low heat. After 15 minutes all the water should be absorbed. Remove from the heat and loosen the grains with a fork. Serve immediately.

TOMATOES

Tomatoes - or "love apples" - were first brought to Europe from their native South America by explorers who prized their attractive colour and delicious flavour.

Today the best tomatoes are the home-grown ones, which are at their prime during the summer months. There is a choice of many varieties, ranging from the small, red or yellow cherry tomato to the large, flat Mediterranean tomato, which is ideal for stuffing. Green tomatoes, available in the autumn, are marvellous for pickles and chutneys.

Whatever type you choose, always ensure that the fruit is firm, bright in colour and regular in shape. The skin should be matt. Avoid any tomatoes which are bruised or cracked.

Tomatoes need little preparation beyond washing, or peeling and seeding when used for cooking. They are delicious simply seasoned and eaten, or sliced and marinated in olive oil and herbs. Otherwise, try them in a cold summer soup or filled or simply made into a thirst-quenching juice. You could also just use them as a garnish to add a touch of colour to any dish.

Any way you choose, they will add few calories to your meal, but lots of vitamins A and C.

Tomato Coulis

INGREDIENTS
6 large ripe tomatoes
2 tbsp vegetable oil (preferably olive oil)
1 shallot or ¼ onion, peeled and finely chopped
1 clove garlic, peeled and crushed
1 tsp tomato puree
salt & freshly ground pepper

METHOD

Remove the "eyes" from the tomatoes with a small knife and make a cross at either end.

Place in a bowl. Bring a kettle of water to the boil and pour the water over the tomatoes until they are completely covered. Leave for about 15 seconds. Remove with a perforated spoon and place in a bowl of iced water. Leave for a few seconds, then peel.

Cut the tomatoes in half horizontally and use a teaspoon to scoop out the seeds and liquid from inside the tomatoes. Discard the seeds and liquid. Then chop the tomatoes coarsely and set aside.

Heat the oil on a medium heat, add the onions and garlic and sweat until transparent but without colouring. Add the tomato puree and sweat for 1 minute. Add the diced tomato and simmer for about 40 minutes, uncovered, until you are left with a thickish coulis.

Season with salt and pepper and remove from the heat.

Liquidise and leave to cool.

Place in a plastic container and freeze until required.

TOMATO COULIS

In many cookery books you will read about "coulis". These are simply fruit or vegetable purees, which can be used hot or cold. They are easy to prepare, and can be frozen to use when required. In summer when tomatoes are at the height of their season, this is an ideal method to capture their flavour for use during the winter months.

Tomato and Aubergine Salad with Basil (top) &
Tomato Filled with Smoked Haddock and Turmeric (below)

Tomato Filled with Smoked Haddock and Turmeric

Serves 4

CALORIES
Approximately 130 per portion

INGREDIENTS
6 tbsp long grain rice
5 oz/150 g fillet of smoked haddock
12 fl oz/350 ml milk
12 fl oz/350 ml water
8 large tomatoes
1 tbsp vegetable oil
1 shallot or ¼ onion, peeled and finely chopped
1 clove garlic, peeled and crushed
½ tsp turmeric
1 large tomato, peeled, deseeded and coarsely chopped
1 tsp capers
3 tbsp single cream
1 tsp parsley, chopped
salt & freshly ground pepper

OVEN TEMPERATURE
180°C/350°F/Gas Mark 4

METHOD
Cook the rice in boiling salted water. Cool under cold water. Drain and keep aside.

Cook the haddock in the milk and water in a shallow pan for about 6-8 minutes. Remove the pan from the heat and leave to cool.

Remove the skin from the fish and flake the flesh. Keep aside. Slice the tops from the tomatoes. Scoop out and discard the seeds. Keep the tomatoes aside.

Heat the oil in a non-stick pan. Add the shallots or onion and garlic and sweat until transparent, but without colouring. Add the turmeric and sweat for a few seconds. Add the diced tomato and cook for 4-5 minutes. Add the capers, rice, haddock and cream. Season with salt and pepper. Add the chopped parsley.

TO FINISH OFF
Spoon the mixture into the tomatoes and place them on a baking tray. Bake in the oven for about 10 minutes. Remove and serve.

Tomato and Aubergine Salad with Basil

Serves 2

CALORIES
Approximately 560 per portion

INGREDIENTS
1 aubergine, medium size
flour to dust aubergine
3 tbsp vegetable oil
salt & freshly ground pepper
1 large tomato

DRESSING
2 tbsp red or white wine vinegar
½ clove garlic, peeled and crushed
6 tbsp olive or vegetable oil
¼ tsp basil, chopped

METHOD
Mix together the dressing ingredients and keep aside.

Top and tail the aubergine and cut into ⅛ in/3 mm thick slices.

Dust with flour and pan-fry in vegetable oil until golden brown and cooked.

Season with salt and freshly ground pepper. Remove from the pan and keep aside.

Cut the tomato into ⅛ in/3 mm slices.

Arrange alternate slices of aubergine and tomato in a circle (the slices should overlap each other) until they are all used up.

Pour the dressing over the slices and leave to marinate for about 20 minutes.

OPTIONAL
Feta cheese, cut into cubes ½ in/1 cm thick and olives would enhance this dish.

MACKEREL

Although mackerel are available throughout the year, they are at their best in the spring. The mackerel is a round, slender fish with a beautiful, silvery blue and green skin. It has no scales, but a bright sheen, which disappears as the fish grows stale. It is an oily, salt water fish with firm, reddish flesh of high quality and with a delicious flavour.

Fresh mackerel can be purchased whole or filleted. Preferably, the fish should be used on the day of purchase: the oil content, which makes the flesh so delicious to eat, also causes the fish to spoil quickly.

Mackerel are excellent eaten freshly grilled, but there are many other ways of cooking them: baked or, in the summer, on the barbecue. Try this quick and tasty way of preparing fresh mackerel: buy a small one from the fishmonger and ask to have it filleted with the head, tail and fins cut off. Season with salt and freshly ground white pepper and dust with flour. Grill for approximately 5-6 minutes on each side until cooked. Sprinkle with freshly chopped herbs, such as dill, parsley and fennel - a squeeze of lemon juice would also enhance the flavour - and serve.

Alternatively mackerel can be bought smoked and ready for eating. For the best flavour, take them out of the fridge 30 minutes before using or just warm under the grill for 30 seconds.

Simply serve with new Jersey potatoes and a sour cream dressing, or try flavouring a mayonnaise sauce with horseradish, grain mustard and chopped walnuts.

Mackerel with Tomato and Olives

Serves 4

CALORIES
Approximately 250 per portion

INGREDIENTS
4 mackerel fillets, each about 4 oz/100 g
3 tsp olive oil
1 oz/25 g butter
1 clove garlic, peeled and crushed
4 medium tomatoes, peeled, deseeded and diced
8 pitted black or green olives, cut into rings
juice of half a lemon
½ tbsp parsley, chopped
chopped basil
salt & freshly ground white pepper

METHOD
Season the mackerel fillets with salt and freshly ground white pepper. Use a sharp knife to make one or two ½ inch (1.25 cm) cuts through the skin down the centre of the fillet. This will prevent them from curling up when cooking.

Heat the oil in a non-stick pan. Place the mackerel fillets (skin side first) in the pan and fry until golden brown. They might still curl a little. Turn over and finish frying. Remove from the pan and keep warm.

Using the same pan, add butter and cook until it starts to "foam". Add the garlic and olive rings. Add the diced tomato and heat for just a minute.

Season with salt and pepper. Add the lemon juice, chopped parsley and basil.

TO FINISH OFF
Place the fish on a serving dish. Spoon the sauce over and serve.

Mackerel and Cream Cheese Pâté in Smoked Salmon

Serves 6

CALORIES
Approximately 510 per portion

INGREDIENTS
12 oz/350 g smoked salmon, sliced
12 oz/350 g smoked mackerel, skinned
6 oz/175 g butter, room temperature
4 oz/100 g cream cheese
juice of half a lemon
salt & freshly ground white pepper
fresh chopped dill

GARNISH
lumpfish or salmon roe
chervil

METHOD
Line 6 ramekin dishes (2¾ in/7 cm in diameter and 1½ in/4 cm deep) completely with smoked salmon. Keep on one side.

Put the mackerel, butter, cream cheese and lemon juice in a blender or food processor and mix until smooth. Taste and season with salt and freshly ground pepper. Add the chopped dill and fold into the mixture.

Spoon into the ramekin dishes (or use a piping bag). Fold over the overlapping edges of the smoked salmon and chill in the refrigerator overnight.

TO FINISH OFF
Turn out the salmon parcels from the ramekin dishes at least 30 minutes before serving to soften the filling.

Garnish with salmon or lumpfish roe and the chervil. Serve with warm toast, Melba toast or brown bread and butter.

If you like, try some of the following alternative garnishes:

Place a few mixed salad leaves around the salmon parcel and serve with vinaigrette.

Instead of lumpfish or salmon roe, simply garnish with a slice of hard-boiled egg with a slice of stuffed olive on top.

Cut a cucumber into thin slices and place them in the centre of a plate in a circle larger than the ramekin dish. Place the parcel on top and garnish with fresh herbs.

PREPARING MACKEREL
In your preparation use acidity, such as lemon juice, vinegar or wine, to counteract the richness of the fish.

PEELING A TOMATO
For some, peeling a tomato might seem like an impossible task. Try the following method and it will seem quite simple. Make sure that the tomato is ripe but not soft. Use a small, sharp knife to remove the "eye" and make a small "X" on the other end of the tomato. Place in a bowl and cover completely with boiling water for 30 seconds. Remove and plunge immediately into a bowl of ice-cold water. The skin will now come off quickly and smoothly.

Mackerel and Cream Cheese Pâté in Smoked Salmon (top) &
Mackerel with Tomato and Olives (below)

CARROTS

arrots are among the most nourishing (particularly high in vitamin A) and inexpensive vegetables. Most often used in savoury dishes, to flavour stocks, sauces, soups and stews, carrots are once again finding their way into sweeter dishes too - in the past they were highly valued for their sweetness.

Although carrots are in the shops all year round, my favourite young, home-grown carrots are available in spring and early summer. These are traditionally sold in bunches with the foliage intact, although, like the larger main crop and finger carrots, they can now also be bought loose or vacuum packed. Young carrots are tender and only need washing before use - older ones may require scraping and peeling. But, as with most vegetables, much of the goodness is in the skin and just below, so always remove less rather than more.

The versatile carrot can be used alone or combined with other foods in both sweet and savoury dishes. Use simply cooked as a vegetable, raw in salads, as a "nibble" with a dip or as the main ingredient of a warm winter or cold summer soup. Carrot is also a colourful garnish for any dish.

Chicken Casserole with Port Wine and Spring Carrots

Chicken Casserole with Port Wine and Spring Carrots

Serves 4

CALORIES
Approximately 450 per portion

INGREDIENTS
4 medium chicken thighs (or 2 per person if you are feeling hungry)
flour to dust the chicken
2 tbsp vegetable oil

SAUCE
1 oz/25 g butter
2 shallots, finely chopped
1 small carrot, peeled and diced
½ clove garlic, peeled and finely chopped
4 button mushrooms, cut in half
4 fl oz/100 ml red wine
4 fl oz/100 ml port wine
17 fl oz/500 ml chicken stock
small sprig rosemary
salt & freshly ground white pepper
½ tsp corn starch, dissolved in a little red wine

GARNISH
8 small spring carrots, cooked in salt water and refreshed under cold water
8 small onions, cooked in salt water and refreshed under cold water
4 rashers bacon, cut into strips (optional)
¼ oz/5 g chopped herbs (parsley, chervil)

OVEN TEMPERATURE
180°C/350°F/Gas Mark 4

METHOD

Season the chicken with salt and pepper and dust lightly with flour.

Heat the oil in a frying pan and brown the chicken all over.

Remove the chicken and transfer to an ovenproof dish.

Cover with a lid and cook in the oven for about 5 minutes.

SAUCE:

Take the pan used to brown the chicken and add butter.

Add the shallots, carrot and garlic and cook until golden brown.

Add the button mushrooms. Add the red wine and boil quickly, reducing the liquid to half the quantity.

Add the port wine and boil quickly, reducing the liquid to half the quantity.

Add the chicken stock and bring the mixture to the boil.

Add the rosemary. Season lightly with salt and pepper.

Pour the sauce over the chicken and return to the oven. Simmer for about 15-20 minutes until cooked.

Whilst the chicken is cooking, prepare the spring carrots and onions for garnish.

TO FINISH OFF

Remove the chicken from the oven. Take out the chicken pieces and keep them warm in a serving dish.

Pass the sauce through a sieve into a saucepan, bring to the boil and reduce the liquid to half the quantity again (skim if necessary).

Season with salt and pepper.

Whisk in the dissolved corn starch and bring to the boil. Pour the sauce over the chicken and keep warm.

Heat a non-stick pan. Add the strips of bacon and cook until crisp. Sprinkle them over the chicken and keep warm.

Add the button onions and carrots to the same pan and heat through. Place on top of the casserole.

Season with salt and pepper and garnish with chopped herbs.

CARROT JUICE
Give yourself an instant health boost: drink a glass of fresh carrot juice. Wash a few carrots and remove the ends. Cut into very fine slices, blend in a food processor and add a little water. Finally, press through a sieve to extract the juice.

PLAICE

Plaice is widely available in this country. It belongs to the flat fish family and has a greyish-brown skin with bright orange spots and soft textured flesh. The large and medium fish are mainly used filleted, whilst the smallest ones can be used whole for sautéeing. Make sure that you buy your fish from a reliable shop and that it is really fresh. If you buy the plaice from a fishmonger and you are thinking of using the fish whole, ask for the black skin and head to be removed. Otherwise ask for fillets, but, if possible, keep the bones and use them to produce your own fish stock and sauce to give your dish a really good flavour.

There are many ways to prepare this fish: for example, grilled, sautéed or deep fried, served with a savoury butter or sauce. For the health conscious, the fillets can be poached in a little fish stock and white wine, with chopped, mixed, fresh herbs added at the end.

Ragout of Plaice with Spring Vegetables

Serves 4

CALORIES
Approximately 425 per portion

INGREDIENTS
16 medium fillets of plaice (1 lb 7 oz/650 g)

SAUCE
1 oz/25 g butter
1 shallot or ¼ onion, peeled and finely chopped
4 fl oz/100 ml dry white wine
12 fl oz/350 ml fish stock
7 fl oz/200 ml double cream
1 tsp dill, finely chopped
salt & freshly ground white pepper
1 tsp whipped cream (optional)

GARNISH
1 oz/25 g butter
Small amount of:
baby carrots
mangetout
baby corn
fine asparagus cut into 2 in (5 cm) pieces
(or your choice of any other spring vegetables)
fresh dill

METHOD
Cut the fish fillets across into finger-size strips. Season with salt and pepper. Keep to one side.

SAUCE
Heat the butter in a saucepan. Add the shallot or onion and sweat until transparent but without colouring. Add the white wine and boil rapidly. Reduce to half the quantity. Add the fish stock and boil rapidly. Reduce to half the quantity.

Add the cream and boil, whisking constantly until a creamy consistency is obtained. Season with salt and pepper. Pass through a sieve into a saucepan and keep to one side.

GARNISH
Place the vegetables separately in boiling, salted water until cooked. Rinse them under cold running water. Drain and keep to one side.

TO FINISH OFF
Bring the sauce back to the boil (if you wish to make the sauce "foamy" add whipped cream to it) and add the fish strips. Simmer for about 2 minutes until the fish is cooked. Do not overcook the fish, as it is very delicate and tends to break up easily.

Remove from the heat and add the chopped dill. Heat the vegetables in butter in a frying pan and season. Serve the fish on plates or in a bowl. Arrange the vegetables on top and garnish with dill.

SUBSTITUTE
Plaice can be substituted for the more expensive sole in most recipes. But remember, it's a fish that is extremely delicate, so always avoid overcooking.

Fillet of Plaice with a Brioche and Herb Crust

Serves 4

CALORIES
Approximately 360 calories per portion

INGREDIENTS
1 tbsp vegetable oil
8 large fillets of plaice, skinned (each about 3½ oz/80 g)
2 oz/50 g butter, room temperature
½ tsp chervil, chopped
¼ tsp dill, chopped
¼ tsp parsley, chopped
1½ oz/40 g white brioche crumbs or white breadcrumbs
salt & freshly ground white pepper

SAUCE
1 tbsp olive oil or vegetable oil
1 shallot or ¼ onion, finely chopped
1 clove garlic, peeled and crushed
1 large red pepper, deseeded and cut into ½ in/1 cm cubes
2 medium-sized tomatoes, peeled and deseeded
4 fl oz/100 ml dry white wine
10 fl oz/300 ml fish stock
sprig of thyme
salt & freshly ground white pepper

OVEN TEMPERATURE
200°C/400°F/Gas Mk 6

METHOD

Heat the oil in a saucepan. Sweat the shallot or onion until transparent but without colouring. Add the garlic, peppers and tomatoes, then the white wine and fish stock and sprig of thyme. Bring to the boil and cover.

Cook on medium heat, stirring constantly, until the peppers are fully cooked. Remove from the heat, remove the sprig of thyme and liquidise.

Pass through a sieve into a saucepan, making sure you use all the puree in the sieve. Bring to the boil and reduce to a thick consistency. Season with salt and freshly ground pepper. Keep to one side.

Place the fillets of fish in front of you. Fold each tail end towards the centre, ensuring that each folded fillet is about the same size.

Season with salt and white pepper. Heat the oil in a non-stick pan and brown the fillets on both sides. Remove from the pan and keep to one side. Cool.

Whisk the butter until a smooth texture is obtained. Keep to one side.

Mix the brioche crumbs with the chopped herbs. Using a brush, cover the fillets with butter, so that you have a coating on top.

Sprinkle the bread and herb mixture on top of the fish fillets and press down lightly with your hand. Butter an ovenproof dish and place the fish in it. Cook in a pre-heated oven for 5-6 minutes. If necessary, flash under a pre-heated grill to brown the crust.

TO FINISH OFF

Arrange the fish on a plate or dish, and pour sauce around. If the sauce is too thick, add some fish stock. Or if the sauce is too thin, just cook it a few minutes longer.

Fish Stock

INGREDIENTS

1¾ lb (800 g) fishbones (sole, turbot, etc) from your fishmonger
1 tbsp margarine
2 shallots or 1 small onion, peeled and chopped
1 clove garlic, peeled and crushed
1 small carrot
1 small piece celery
18 fl oz (500 ml) dry white wine
1¾ pt (1 ltr) water
3 white peppercorns, crushed
1 bayleaf
sprig of thyme and dill

In many of my recipes I refer to stocks. Although you are able to buy them, home-made will generally have a far superior flavour and it is quite simple if you make large quantities at one time, reduce, then pour into ice trays and freeze. When frozen, place in bags and store in the freezer until required. The following recipe will give 1¾ pints (1 litre), which should be reduced to half for freezing:

METHOD

Wash the bones with cold water and drain. Warm the margarine in a stockpot. Sweat the vegetables, add the fishbones and wine and bring to the boil. Add the remaining ingredients, bring back to the boil and simmer for 30 minutes, without covering. Remove scum as necessary with a perforated ladle.
Pass through a muslin cloth, using a ladle, and allow to cool.

LAMB

Lamb is a favourite in many British homes. In fact, as a nation, the British are amongst the highest consumers of lamb in the world. Fresh, home-produced lamb, particularly "new season", is considered to be of the very best quality. By mid-spring it is available in most shops, but still fairly high in price. As the season progresses, the amount of lamb available increases and prices drop accordingly.

Lamb has a delicate flavour and high nutritional value. Not only is it an excellent source of protein, it also provides iron and other minerals and is rich in vitamins. So, not only does it taste delicious, but it's also good for you.

Lamb varies in colour according to age and breed. Generally, top quality lamb has pale pink, velvety flesh with fat that is firm and white.

The flesh of older animals grows darker and the fat creamy, then yellow. Although the fat is a useful judge of quality, it is considered unhealthy eating. Therefore, you should always trim away as much as possible before using.

There are many different cuts available ranging in price according to "choice". Think before you buy! While the "choice" cuts are popular, the less expensive ones are just as nourishing and delicious with the proper preparation. If you are not sure of what to buy, a good butcher will be happy to advise you.

Skewers of Lamb Marinated with Ginger and Soya

Serves 2 (1½ skewers per person)

CALORIES
Approximately 225 per skewer

INGREDIENTS
3 wooden or metal skewers
(if wooden, soak in water for 10 minutes to prevent them from burning when cooking)

7 oz/200 g lean shoulder or leg of lamb (no bones, skin and fat removed) cut into
1¼ in/3 cm cubes
(For each skewer you need about 5 pieces of meat)

1 medium-sized pepper (red, yellow or green), stalk and seeds removed
1 medium-sized onion, peeled

MARINADE
2 tbsp sesame or vegetable oil
½ clove garlic, peeled and finely chopped
½ tsp light soya sauce
1 pinch thyme, finely chopped
1 pinch ginger powder or freshly chopped ginger
salt & freshly ground pepper

GARNISH
1 lemon, cut in half

METHOD:

MARINADE
Mix together all the ingredients except the salt in a bowl. Add the lamb cubes to the marinade and mix well. Cover with clingfilm and leave in the refrigerator overnight.

PEPPER AND ONION
Cut the pepper into 1¼ in/3 cm cubes.

Cut the onion in half lengthwise and and then cut each piece again crosswise (so that you get pieces which are almost square).

Cook the pepper and onion pieces in salted water for 40 seconds. Remove and refresh in ice cold water. Drain. Dry on a kitchen towel.

DRESSING THE SKEWER
Pierce one piece of meat onto the skewer followed by a piece of onion and a piece of pepper. Continue until all the meat cubes are used up, but make sure that they are not pressed too tightly against each other. Keep to one side.

TO FINISH OFF
Season with salt and cook on a barbecue for about 6-8 minutes until medium cooked OR place on a tray and grill for 5-6 minutes OR pan-fry in a non-stick pan by sealing off the meat on all sides, then reducing the heat and frying until golden brown and medium cooked.

Dress on a plate or serving dish and serve with half a lemon.

Rack of English Lamb with a Grain Mustard and Herb Crust

Serves 2

CALORIES
Approximately 580 per portion

INGREDIENTS
1 lb/450 g rack of lamb, trimmed and sinews removed

1 tsp vegetable oil

salt & freshly ground white pepper

HERB CRUST
½ clove garlic, peeled and finely chopped

1 oz/25 g white breadcrumbs (preferably brioche crumbs)

½ tsp each: parsley; thyme; chervil; tarragon, all finely chopped

1 tsp grain mustard

1 tbsp white wine

SAUCE
1 tsp vegetable oil

1 shallot or ¼ onion, peeled and finely chopped

2 fl oz/50 ml red port wine

7 fl oz/200 ml lamb stock, reduced

salt & freshly ground white pepper

1 pinch cornflour, dissolved in a little water

OVEN TEMPERATURE
180°C/350°F/Gas Mark 4

(Finish off under the grill on a high temperature).

METHOD:

HERB CRUST
Mix the garlic, herbs and breadcrumbs together in a bowl and keep to one side.

SAUCE
Sweat the shallot in vegetable oil in a saucepan until transparent, but without colouring.

Add the port wine and cook the liquid to half the quantity.

Add the lamb stock and cook the liquid to half the quantity. Season. Add the dissolved cornflour and bring to the boil for 2 minutes. Pass through a sieve into a saucepan and keep to one side.

LAMB
Season the lamb with salt and pepper. Heat the oil in a roasting tray and brown the rack of lamb on both sides.

Roast in the oven for about 10-15 minutes (basting once or twice) and then rest in a warm place for 3 minutes.

TO FINISH OFF
Mix the mustard and wine and brush the rack of lamb.

Sprinkle the herb mixture on top of the rack and brown under the grill.

Place on a serving dish and serve. The sauce should be served separately.

Braised Shoulder of Lamb with Rosemary

Serves 2

CALORIES
Approximately 490 per portion

INGREDIENTS
half shoulder of lamb
1 tbsp olive or vegetable oil
4 whole garlic cloves, peeled
3 sprigs fresh rosemary (or 2 tsp dried)
2 fresh basil leaves (or 1 tsp dried)
1 medium-sized potato, cut into
1½ in/4 cm cubes
6 shallots, peeled
2 fl oz/50 ml white wine
5 fl oz/150 ml lamb stock
salt & freshly ground pepper

OVEN TEMPERATURE
180°C/350°F/Gas Mark 4

METHOD

Heat the oil in a non-stick pan. Add the garlic, rosemary and basil and brown until golden. Remove from the heat.

Season the lamb with salt and pepper and place in a casserole dish. Spoon the herb mixture on top. Add the potato cubes and shallots to the casserole dish.

Add the wine and lamb stock and bring to the boil. Cover with a lid and cook in the oven for about 1½ hours, or until cooked. Check after 1 hour and add more lamb stock if necessary to prevent burning.

The roast should be golden brown and tender. Also note that there will not be a lot of sauce left in your pan at the end.

TO FINISH OFF

Serve straight from the dish, or remove the lamb and place on a serving dish with the onions and potatoes.

Rack of English Lamb with a Grain Mustard and Herb Crust

MARINATE LAMB FOR TENDERNESS

Make sure the meat you use is not too fresh. Preferably buy your meat 2 or 3 days before required.

Trim off all surplus fat and marinate in a mixture of vegetable oil, crushed garlic, thyme, rosemary and freshly ground pepper.

Cover with clingfilm or foil and keep in the coldest part of the refrigerator until required (maximum 3 days). This will not only enhance the flavour of the lamb, but it will also increase tenderness.

SALMON

almon is considered by many to be the very best of all fish. Certainly, seen swimming in the water, or when freshly caught, it is a handsome fish, with bright, silvery scales and red gills.

But it is not for its looks that salmon is so highly prized: it is the firm, oily, pink-red flavourful flesh that earns salmon its reputation.

Salmon is a salt water fish, which is born in and returns to the rivers to spawn. It is now available to buy throughout the year from many different countries, but the British season for salmon is in its peak from May to July, when salmon are caught in the cool, fast-flowing rivers.

Salmon is not only delicious eaten fresh, but it is also considered a delicacy smoked. Its high fat content makes it an ideal fish for this method of preparation.

As an alternative to smoked salmon, try Salmon Carpaccio: cut a salmon fillet on a slight angle, as thinly as possible, then spread on a dish to marinate in 2 tsp nut oil, 3 tsp lime juice, salt and pepper.

Refrigerate for about 1 hour. To serve, sprinkle with chopped walnuts and dill. Eat with brown bread and butter.

Baked Salmon Steaks

Serves 2

CALORIES
Approximately 585 per portion (with sauce)

INGREDIENTS
2 salmon steaks (each 6 oz/175 g)

1 tsp mild mustard

salt & freshly ground white pepper

2 tbsp butter, at room temperature

2 oz/50 g carrots cut into fine 2 in/5 cm strips, cooked for about 30 seconds and refreshed in cold water

2 oz/50 g leeks, white part (2 in/5 cm long)

2 sprigs fresh dill

SAUCE
7 fl oz/200 ml dry white wine

4 fl oz/100 ml fish or vegetable stock

4 fl oz/100 ml single cream

2 tsp butter

2 tsp flour

salt & freshly ground white pepper

2 tbsp herbs, chopped - e.g. dill, parsley, chives

(The sauce is optional and can be replaced with a mayonnaise, hollandaise sauce or sabayon)

OVEN TEMPERATURE
200°C/400°F/Gas Mk 6

METHOD:

SALMON
Place salmon steaks on a plate. Brush lightly with mustard. Season with salt and freshly ground pepper.

Brush two pieces of greaseproof paper (12 x 10 in/30 x 25 cm) on the inside with butter.

Season the carrots and leeks separately. Place carrots and leeks on one half of the greaseproof paper. Place the salmon steaks on top. Garnish with the dill sprigs on top of the fish. To close the parcel, fold the other side loosely over the fish and fold the edges together several times to secure. A paper clip or staple can be used if necessary.

Place the parcels on a baking tray in a pre-heated oven and bake for about 15 minutes, depending upon the thickness.

SAUCE
Mix the butter with the flour until you have a smooth paste. Cook the white wine and stock on a high heat and reduce to half the quantity. Add the cream and bring to the boil. Add the flour and butter mixture, stirring constantly. Boil for 4-5 minutes until a creamy consistency is obtained. Season with salt and white pepper. Add the chopped herbs. Serve in a pre-heated sauceboat.

TO FINISH OFF
Remove the paper parcels from the oven and place on a pre-heated plate. The parcels should be cut open at the table - the aroma is mouth-watering.
Serve the sauce separately, or, alternatively, serve with half a lemon.

Boiled new Jersey potatoes are a good accompaniment to the dish.

Puff Pastry Case with a Ragout of Salmon in a Saffron and Lime Sauce

Puff Pastry Case with a Ragout of Salmon in a Saffron and Lime Sauce

Serves 2

CALORIES
Approximately 520 per portion

INGREDIENTS
*2 puff pastry cases (pre-baked or frozen) OR
3 oz/75 g puff pastry (and a little flour for
dusting)*

1 tbsp vegetable oil

*7 oz/200 g fillet of salmon (no skin), cut into
½ in/1 cm cubes*

salt & freshly ground white pepper

SAUCE
*Use the same basic recipe as for the sauce
with Baked Salmon Steaks on page 66, but
replace the herbs with a pinch of saffron
powder or shreds of saffron and ½ tsp of
lime juice*

GARNISH
1 sprig dill

*1 medium-size tomato, peeled, deseeded and
diced (optional)*

OVEN TEMPERATURE
180°C/350°F/Gas Mark 4

METHOD

Use the prepared puff pastry cases and bake as directed, or, if you prefer, prepare your own.

Proceed as follows: Dust the puff pastry with flour. Roll out the pastry to a thickness of ⅛ in/3 mm. Cut into 2 rectangles 3½ x 2¼ in/9 x 6 cm. Allow to rest for 30 minutes in the fridge.

Mark out a lid with a sharp knife, without cutting all the way through the pastry, leaving a small border all the way round the edge of the case.

Place on a baking tray and cook for about 15 minutes until golden brown.

Cut out the pre-marked lid. Remove and keep aside in a warm place.

SAUCE

Follow the instructions in the recipe for the sauce served with Baked Salmon Steaks. At the end add a pinch of saffron powder and lime juice to taste. Keep aside.

TO FINISH OFF

Season the salmon cubes with salt and pepper. Heat the vegetable oil in a non-stick pan and fry the salmon until golden brown and cooked.

Remove and drain on a kitchen towel. Place the puff pastry cases on a dish and fill with the cooked salmon cubes.

Pour the sauce carefully over the fish and garnish with the pastry lid and a sprig of dill and diced tomatoes.

POACHING SALMON

If you are thinking of poaching a whole fish, perhaps for a party, remember always start off with a cold stock. This needs to be prepared beforehand with the following ingredients:

1 onion; 1 small carrot; 1 small white leek, cut into pieces; a bayleaf; a sprig of dill and thyme; 4 crushed peppercorns; 7 fl oz/200 ml white wine, 1¾ pints/1 litre water; 2 tbsp salt.

Bring all the ingredients to the boil and simmer for 20 minutes. Leave to cool. When cold, place the whole fish in it and slowly bring to the boil. Reduce heat and poach. If you have steaks or fillets, use the same stock, but hot: bring to the boil, place the steak in it and poach for 5-10 minutes.

Cooking times for whole salmon:
up to 2lb: 15 minutes per lb
up to 5lb: 10 minutes per lb
over 5lb: 8 minutes per lb

SALADS

Long gone are the days when "salad" meant lettuce, tomato and cucumber! Today the endless variety of ingredients available makes salad a suitable and sophisticated addition to any meal. Starter, simple side-dish or mouth-watering main course - the choice is yours. With such a host of products available, such contrasting colours, flavours and textures, the only limitation is imagination!

In the summer ingredients become cheaper, but all year round salads provide an excellent source of nutrition, so get into the salad habit. Salads are a particularly good source of minerals, vitamins and fibre. Many are ideal for slimmers, too - but for those of you with an eye on your weight, watch out for calorie-laden dressings and ingredients such as cheese, nuts and avocado.

From a simple combination of different types of leaves, to a more complex concoction, one of the most important ingredients is the dressing.

A basic oil and vinegar dressing (2-3 parts oil; 1 part vinegar) will enhance most salads. Mix and match oils and vinegars to suit your taste: try olive, sesame or walnut oil and red or white wine or raspberry vinegar. Honey, garlic, herbs and fruit juices also make for interesting flavours.

For the health-conscious, try low-fat yoghurt with lemon juice and herbs. Experiment to develop a new flavour to suit your personal taste.

Salads can be prepared partially in advance, but most should be dressed at the last minute. And, of course, there's seldom a need to keep salads hot. So not only are they fun to prepare, nutritious and delicious, but they also make life particularly easy when entertaining.

Warm Spinach, Chicken Liver and Bacon Salad with a Herb and Sesame Dressing

Serves 4

CALORIES
Approximately 310 per portion

INGREDIENTS
8 oz/225 g young spinach leaves

7 oz/200 g chicken livers, trimmed (large ones cut in half)

4 rashers streaky bacon, cut into strips about ¼ in/1 cm long

1½ oz/40 g unsalted butter

5 sprigs rosemary

DRESSING
1 tbsp white wine vinegar

juice of half a lemon passed through a sieve

2 tbsp light soya sauce

½ clove garlic, peeled and chopped

2 tbsp sesame oil

1 tbsp sunflower oil

2 tbsp water

1 pinch ground cardamom

¼ tbsp basil, chopped

½ tbsp chives, chopped

salt & freshly ground white pepper

METHOD
To prepare the dressing for the salad, mix together the vinegar, lemon juice and soya sauce. Add the garlic, both oils and the water. Season with salt, freshly ground white pepper and cardamom to taste. Mix for a few seconds with a hand blender until homogenised. Add the chopped basil and chives.

Stem and wash the spinach leaves. Tear any large pieces into smaller ones.

Season the chicken livers and keep aside. Heat a non-stick pan and add the bacon strips. Pan-fry until crisp. Remove and drain. Using the same pan, add the butter and heat until golden brown. Add 1 sprig of rosemary. Then add the chicken livers and cook until they are lightly browned on all sides, but still slightly pink inside. Remove from the pan and drain. Discard the rosemary sprig.

TO FINISH OFF
Mix the warm chicken livers and bacon with some of the dressing.

Mix the spinach leaves with the remaining dressing. Arrange the spinach on 4 plates.

Divide the warm chicken liver and bacon mixture between the 4 plates on top of the spinach. Garnish each with a sprig of rosemary and serve.

Pickled Herring Salad (left) & Warm Spinach, Chicken Liver and Bacon Salad with a Herb and Sesame Dressing (right)

Pickled Herring Salad

Serves 4

CALORIES
Approximately 530 per portion

INGREDIENTS
1 Golden Delicious apple
7 oz/200 g new potatoes, cooked and peeled
4 oz/100 g beetroot, cooked
2 gherkins
4 pieces pickled herring

DRESSING
3 tbsp gherkin juice
1 tbsp white wine vinegar
8 tbsp vegetable oil
½ tsp English mustard
½ tsp horseradish
1 tsp dill, chopped
2 tbsp quark or cottage cheese

GARNISH
mixed salad leaves, washed
2 hard-boiled eggs
dill

METHOD
Remove the core of the apple and cut into ½ in/1 cm pieces.

Cut the potatoes, beetroot, gherkin and herring into pieces the same size. Mix these together in a bowl.

DRESSING
Mix together all the ingredients for the dressing. Season with salt and pepper.

TO FINISH OFF
Mix the dressing with all the other ingredients.

Arrange on a plate with salad leaves. Garnish with dill and egg slices or quark.

Summer Salad with Sweetbread and Vegetables

Serves 2

CALORIES
Approximately 325 per portion

INGREDIENTS
7 oz/200 g calf's sweetbread
1 tbsp vegetable oil
3 tsp flour to dust sweetbread
salt & freshly ground pepper

VEGETABLES AND SALAD
3 oz/75 g of any salad leaves in season (curly endive, raddichio, mache, spinach, etc.)
7 oz/200 g French beans, topped, tailed and cut in half
1 small carrot, peeled
1 spring onion, cut into ⅛ in/3 mm rings

DRESSING
2 tsp honey
1 tbsp cooking liquid from vegetables
1 tbsp sherry vinegar
2 tbsp walnut or vegetable oil
salt & freshly ground pepper
½ tsp chives, chopped

METHOD
Soak the sweetbread in cold water overnight. Use a knife to remove the skin, then break the sweetbread into small rosettes and dry on a kitchen towel.

VEGETABLES AND SALAD

Wash the salad leaves and keep to one side. Cook the beans in salted water for about 2 minutes (they should still be crisp), refresh in iced water and drain (reserve 1 tbsp of the cooking liquid for the dressing). Keep aside.

Cut the carrots into rings about ⅛ in/3 mm thick. Cook for about 30 seconds, refresh in iced water, drain and keep aside.

DRESSING
Dissolve the honey in the cooking liquid reserved from the beans. Leave to cool and then add all the other dressing ingredients. Keep aside.

TO FINISH OFF
Season the sweetbread with salt and pepper. Dust with flour, shaking off any loose flour. Heat the oil in a non-stick pan. Add the sweetbread pieces and fry until golden brown on all sides. Reduce the heat and continue frying until cooked. Remove from the pan and place on kitchen towel. Keep aside. Mix the salad leaves and vegetables and add the dressing. Place on a serving dish and put the sweetbread pieces on top.

Universal Salad Dressing

INGREDIENTS
½ clove garlic, peeled and finely chopped
1 small shallot or ¼ onion, peeled and finely chopped
2 tbsp white wine vinegar
2 tbsp bouillon
salt & freshly ground white pepper
1 tbsp mayonnaise
1 tsp grain mustard
2 tbsp sunflower oil

METHOD
Boil the garlic and chopped shallots in white wine vinegar and bouillon. Add all the remaining ingredients. Mix quickly with a hand blender. Season with salt and pepper. Add your choice of herbs.

DRESSING SALADS

Most salad ingredients can be prepared in advance and stored in an airtight container for up to 24 hours. But remember, always mix in the dressing at the last moment to avoid loss of taste, texture and colour.

Starchy ingredients, on the other hand, benefit from marinating in a warm dressing to absorb the flavour.

My favourite dressing, provided above, enhances most salads.

CRAB

Crabs are available all year round, but are at their best from May to October. When choosing a crab, look for one of medium size (about 3-4 lbs/1.4-1.8 kg) and ensure that both claws are attached. Remember, the meat is of two types: in the legs and claws you'll find it is white and delicately flavoured, whilst in the body you'll find the creamy-brown, stronger flavoured flesh. Male crabs can be distinguished by their larger claws and thus provide more white meat, but in the female, you'll often find a delicate edible roe. If you have a preference, ask before purchasing.

Whilst crabs can be bought live, and are not difficult to cook, they are time-consuming and quite tricky to prepare for use. If you're not experienced at this, your fishmonger will do it for you. Otherwise, buy the meat fresh and already picked over, or frozen or tinned.

But remember, like all shellfish, crab must be eaten very fresh - always on the day of purchase.

Steamed Crab and Spring Onion in a Lettuce Parcel

Serves 2

CALORIES
Approximately 385 per portion

INGREDIENTS: PARCEL
2 iceberg lettuce leaves, medium size
1 tsp vegetable oil
½ shallot, peeled and finely chopped
¼ clove garlic, peeled and finely chopped
½ spring onion, cut into fine rings
4 oz/100 g crabmeat, white and picked
salt & freshly ground pepper

BUTTER MIXTURE
¼ oz/5 g butter
¼ oz/5 g flour

SAUCE
½ oz/15 g butter
1 shallot, peeled and finely chopped
2 tbsp Noilly Prat (optional)
2 fl oz/50 ml dry white wine
5 fl oz/150 ml fish stock
5 fl oz/150 ml single cream
salt & freshly ground pepper

GARNISH
½ oz/15 g salmon roe
dill
1 medium tomato, peeled, deseeded and diced

OVEN TEMPERATURE
150°C/300°F/Gas Mark 2

METHOD
Cook the iceberg lettuce in salted, boiling water for about 15 seconds. Remove and refresh in iced water. Drain and place on kitchen towel

Line 2 ramekin dishes with clingfilm suitable for food. Cut the stem out of the leaves and line the dishes with the leaves. Keep to one side.

FILLING
Heat the oil in a non-stick pan. Add the shallots and garlic and sweat until transparent, but without colouring. Add the spring onion and crabmeat. Season with salt and pepper. Remove from the heat and leave to cool.

Divide the mixture between the 2 ramekin dishes, pressing down lightly with your fingers. Fold the overlapping lettuce leaves inside. Refrigerate until required.

SAUCE
Mix the butter and flour to make a Beurre Manié. Keep aside. Sweat the shallots in butter until transparent without colouring. Add the Noilly Prat. Add the white wine, boil and reduce to half the quantity.

Add the fish stock, boil and reduce to half the quantity.

Add the cream and bring to the boil. Add the butter and flour mixture and boil until a creamy consistency is obtained. Season with salt and pepper.

TO FINISH OFF
Turn the parcels out of the ramekin dishes onto a buttered piece of tin foil. Remove the clingfilm. Place in a steamer and steam gently for about 8 minutes. Remove carefully and place on a serving dish or plate.

Bring the sauce to the boil and add the diced tomato. Remove from the heat and spoon the sauce around the parcels. Garnish with salmon roe and dill.

Steamed Crab and Spring Onion in a Lettuce Parcel (left) & Crab and Pawpaw Salad (right)

Crab and Pawpaw Salad with Coriander

Serves 4

CALORIES
Approximately 330 per portion

INGREDIENTS
4 oz/125 g mixed salad leaves (e.g. curly endive, oakleaf, mache, radicchio, lollo rosso)

1 small, ripe pawpaw

7 oz/200 g white crabmeat

DRESSING
2 fl oz/50 ml sour cream

4 fl oz/100 ml mayonnaise

1 tsp white wine vinegar

1 tbsp ketchup

1 tsp grated horseradish

1 tbsp orange juice

salt & freshly ground pepper

½ tsp chopped coriander

GARNISH
spring onion and radish, cut into rings

METHOD
Wash and dry the salad leaves. Cut into fine strips and divide between 4 serving plates or bowls. Halve the pawpaw, remove the skin and pips and cut into ½ in/1 cm cubes. Mix with the crabmeat and keep aside.

DRESSING
Mix together the sour cream and mayonnaise. Add the vinegar, ketchup, horseradish and orange juice. Season with salt and pepper. Add the coriander.

TO FINISH OFF
Mix the dressing with the crabmeat and pawpaw. Dress on the salad leaves and garnish with spring onion and radish.

BEURRE MANIÉ
In many recipes I use a mixture of butter and flour to thicken. The professional term for this is Beurre Manié. To make this, use the butter at room temperature and whisk until "white" in colour. Then mix in an equal quantity of flour. Keep in the refrigerator or freezer and use as required to thicken soups or sauces. To use, add approximately 1 tsp of the mixture to 4 fl oz/100 ml boiling liquid and whisk. Boil for 3-4 minutes. If it is not thick enough, add more of the mixture until the desired consistency is obtained.

STRAWBERRIES

Gorgeous strawberries are a favourite fruit the world over - considered by many to be the queen of all berries.

Imported strawberries are available in the UK almost the whole year round. However, although large and attractive to the eye, they often lack flavour, because transportation procedures usually result in imported berries being picked long before they are ripe, when the flavour is still under-developed.

For the strawberry connoisseur, nothing can match the home-grown fruit available from June to August. These ripe, juicy specimens are unbeatable for taste. If you're fortunate enough to grow your own, or live close to a strawberry farm, you can truly enjoy them at their best: freshly picked, perfectly ripe and still warm from the summer sunshine.

The vast majority of us, however, happily make do with those which can be bought in the shops. There are many varieties available, including the wild, small strawberries which abound in Europe. All are very low in calories, as well as being a good source of vitamins (particularly vitamins A and C) and minerals. Use strawberries on the day of purchase. Choose berries that are fresh looking - avoid at all costs fruit which is under-ripe or soft.

Needless to say, they are delicious eaten on their own, traditionally with cream, or, as a healthier alternative, with yoghurt or creme fraiche.

Try the following: cut the strawberries in half, sprinkle with sugar and season with black pepper. Pour single cream on top and leave for about 45 minutes to marinate before serving .They should not be left in the refrigerator.

There are many other methods of preparation, particularly as the season progresses and prices fall.

Try them in cakes, tarts, ice-cream or water ice, or in home-made jam, which will be enjoyed long after the last, fresh, home-grown strawberry has been picked.

Gratinated Strawberries with Grand Marnier

Serves 4

CALORIES
Approximately 145 per portion

INGREDIENTS
1 lb/450 g ripe strawberries, cut in half or quarters depending on size

GRATIN MIXTURE
4 egg yolks (keep the egg white and freeze for other dishes which require egg white)

3 tbsp sugar

4 tbsp single cream

2 tbsp Grand Marnier

½ tsp grated orange zest

TO GARNISH
fresh mint and icing sugar

METHOD
Wash the strawberries and place in an ovenproof dish. Keep to one side.

GRATIN MIXTURE
Mix all the ingredients together in a metal bowl using a whisk.
Place the bowl over a pan of water which is almost simmering, and continue whisking until the mixture is ready - it should be thick and foamy but not too 'runny'. Pour over the strawberries immediately.

TO FINISH OFF
Place the dish under the grill and bake until golden brown.
Using a fine sieve, dust the icing sugar over the dish. Garnish with mint and serve instantly.

This dish is delicious with any ice cream.

STORING STRAWBERRIES

When you buy strawberries, make sure the berries are not bruised or mouldy. If you have bought them in punnets, remove them from their packaging as soon as you can and check that they are all in good condition, then put them in the refrigerator.

If the strawberries are not ripe, leave them outside the refrigerator, preferably in the sunshine, for a couple of hours to ripen.

Strawberries with a Warm Orange and Red Wine Sauce (left) & Gratinated Strawberries with Grand Marnier (right)

Strawberries with a Warm Orange and Red Wine Sauce Flavoured with Lemon Grass

Serves 4

CALORIES
Approximately 230 per portion

INGREDIENTS
7 fl oz/200 ml red wine
4 fl oz/100 ml orange juice
3 tbsp sugar
½ vanilla pod, split in half
1 small piece lemon grass
2 tsp cornflour
2 tsp Grand Marnier
1 lb/450 g ripe strawberries, cut in half
7 oz/200 g vanilla ice-cream
chopped pistachio nuts

METHOD
Mix together the red wine, orange juice, sugar, vanilla pod and lemon grass in a saucepan and bring to the boil.

Dissolve the cornflour in the Grand Marnier.

Add the dissolved cornflour to the red wine mixture and simmer for 2 minutes. Pass through a fine sieve and keep warm.

TO FINISH OFF
Arrange the cut strawberries on plates or in glasses.

Pour the warm sauce over them.

Spoon a scoop of ice-cream on top and garnish with chopped pistachio nuts.

PEAS

Aperennial favourite, peas come in many varieties. In spring and summer fresh green peas and mangetout (snow peas) are popular, whilst many other varieties are dried and make a welcome alternative, particularly in the winter months.

The earliest home-grown peas available are the mangetout. These are immature peas with a crisp, tender pod, which are cooked and - as their French name implies - eaten whole. When buying, look out for small, bright green pods. They are available frozen, but the fresh ones are far superior - so make the most of them when they're in season and less expensive.

Try them crisply blanched in a salad with grilled bacon and raw button mushrooms, or stir-fried in sesame oil together with prawns or slices of chicken, or simply as a vegetable, tossed in butter. They can also be used to add colour and make an attractive garnish when finishing off a dish.

Home-grown green peas are available from about May. They have round, smooth seeds and are best shelled just before cooking. Mature peas have wrinkled seeds and are used for drying. When buying, avoid large pods, particularly if the seeds are showing through. Before you buy, taste one raw; they should be sweet and tender.

Peas, of course, make a popular vegetable, particularly when young and fresh. Older peas make delicious purees or soups - try a cold soup, flavoured with mint, on a warm day.

Marinated Chicken Breast with Mangetout

Serves 2

CALORIES
Approximately 395 per portion

INGREDIENTS

2 chicken breasts, skin removed
2 tbsp sesame or vegetable oil
salt & freshly ground white pepper

MARINADE
2 tbsp light soya sauce
1 pinch chilli powder
½ tsp sherry

VEGETABLES
2 tomatoes, peeled and deseeded
1 yellow pepper, cut in half, seeds removed
4 oz/100 g mangetout, ends removed
1 tbsp sesame or vegetable oil
1 clove garlic, peeled and finely chopped
1 shallot or ¼ onion, peeled and finely chopped
½ tsp coriander, chopped
(keep a few leaves for garnish)

OVEN TEMPERATURE
180°C/350°F/Gas Mark 4

METHOD:

MARINADE
Mix all the marinade ingredients together and marinate the chicken breasts for about 30 minutes.

VEGETABLES
Cut each peeled tomato into six pieces. Cut the pepper into ½ in/1 cm cubes and boil in salted water for 1½ minutes. Remove and refresh in iced water. Drain and keep aside. Cook the mangetout, keeping them crisp, in salted water. Remove and refresh in iced water. Drain.

TO FINISH OFF
Season the chicken with salt and pepper and pan-fry in 1 tbsp oil until golden brown. Transfer to the oven for about 6 minutes until cooked. Keep in a warm place. In the pan heat the remaining oil and sweat the shallots or onion and the garlic until transparent but without colouring. Add the pepper and fry until hot. Add the mangetout and heat for about 30 seconds. Add the tomato. Season with salt and pepper and add the chopped coriander. Arrange the vegetables in a serving dish and place the chicken on top. Garnish with coriander leaves.

> **"REFRESHING"**
> In many of my recipes, I talk of "refreshing" which is the process used to prevent further cooking and to "set" the colour of vegetables. It is used after blanching or cooking in boiling water. To "refresh" remove the vegetables from the boiling water and place immediately in a bowl of ice-cold water. When cold, drain and reserve until required.

Pea Soup with Ham Muffins

Serves 4 (2-3 muffins per person)

CALORIES
Soup: approximately 280 per portion
Muffins: approximately 130 each

INGREDIENTS: SOUP
1 oz/25 g butter

1 shallot or ¼ onion, finely chopped
1 lb/450 g fresh peas
1¼ pt/750 ml chicken or vegetable stock
½ pt/300 ml single cream
salt & pepper
nutmeg

MUFFINS
1 egg (size 3)
4 tbsp vegetable oil
6 oz/175 g diced ham
½ shallot, peeled and finely chopped
5 oz/150 g wholemeal flour
1 heaped tsp baking powder
3 fl oz/75ml milk
pinch salt (do not use if ham is salty)

OVEN TEMPERATURE
200°C/400°F/Gas Mark 6

METHOD:

SOUP
Sweat the shallots in butter until transparent but without colouring.

Add the peas and sweat for a minute.

Add the stock, cover with a lid and boil for 15 minutes.

Add the cream. Blend in a food processor and pour through a sieve into a saucepan.

Bring to the boil, cook for a further 5 minutes and season.

MUFFINS
Mix together the egg, oil, ham and shallot. Keep to one side.

Mix the flour and baking powder and a pinch of salt. Combine the two mixtures by folding together gently. Add the milk gradually, using only as much as is necessary to obtain a "moist" mixture.

Line a fairy cake tin with greaseproof paper cases. Spoon the mixture into the cases and bake for 20 minutes.

Allow to rest for 5 minutes. Remove from cases and serve warm.

Hosting special occasions should be fun for both guests and hosts. However, all too often the host or hostess is trapped in the kitchen preparing food, and, as a result, has little opportunity to enjoy the party to the full.

The two recipes below fit the bill for any special occasion. Not only are they are both attractive and delicious, but also, and equally important, they are very easy to make and can be prepared well in advance the day before you serve them.

So, if you are planning a dinner party or a special lunch and want to spend more time with your guests, give these recipes a try. You won't be disappointed and nor will your guests!

Strawberry Gateau

Serves 6

CALORIES
Approximately 365 per portion

INGREDIENTS
1 vanilla sponge round (7 in/18 cm diameter), bought or home-made
9 oz/250 g strawberries

MOUSSE
1 tsp sugar
11 oz/300 g strawberries
8 fl oz/250 ml semi-whipped double cream
2 egg whites
½ tsp lemon juice
5 level tsp gelatine powder

SYRUP
3 tbsp water
1½ tbsp sugar

GARNISH
5 fl oz/150 ml whipped cream
6 whole small strawberries (from above)
6 sprigs mint

METHOD

Cut the vanilla sponge in half to form two layers, each ⅛ in/4 mm thick. Place one layer in a 7 in/18 cm cake ring.

Keep 6 of the best small strawberries aside for garnish. Cut the remaining strawberries in half and line the inside of the ring. The strawberries should stand upright with their cut edge facing outwards, and they should all be touching each other.

For the mousse, mix the sugar and strawberries. Place in a saucepan and simmer for 4 minutes. Puree and pass through a sieve into a saucepan. Return to simmering point and remove from the heat. Immediately sprinkle over the gelatine and whisk in to dissolve completely. Stir in the lemon juice. Leave to cool, but do not allow to set.

Whip the cream until semi-stiff and add it to the cool fruit puree, using a spatula. Whip the egg white until stiff and fold into the mixture.

Pour the mousse into the centre of the cake ring and add the remaining halved strawberries at the same time.

Place the second half of the sponge on top. Leave to set in the refrigerator for about 3-4 minutes.

For the syrup, mix together the water and sugar. Simmer for 2 minutes. Leave to cool and keep aside.

TO FINISH OFF

Brush the vanilla sponge with the syrup. Whisk the cream and spread evenly on top of the cake. Use a knife to loosen the cake from the ring by cutting around the edge as close to the ring as possible.

Place the cake on a plate and gently remove the ring. Decorate with cream rosettes, mint and the strawberry halves.

Strawberry Gateau

Tartar of Smoked Salmon and Crab

Serves 2

CALORIES
300 per portion

INGREDIENTS

3 oz/75 g white crab meat
3 oz/75 g smoked salmon, diced
1 oz/25 g shallots, peeled and finely chopped
½ tsp white wine vinegar
2 tsp walnut or vegetable oil
salt & pepper
3 oz/75 g crème fraiche

GARNISH

1 cucumber, sliced ¹⁄₁₆ in/2 mm thick
1 tsp salmon roe (optional)
1 tsp lumpfish (optional)
2 sprigs dill (optional)

METHOD

Mix the crab meat, diced smoked salmon and shallots in a bowl.

Mix the vinegar and walnut oil together and add to the salmon mixture. Season with salt and pepper.

Divide into two portions and place into metal rings to shape, or use ramekin dishes. Spread the crème fraiche on top. Cool in the refrigerator.

TO FINISH OFF

Arrange the cucumber slices in circles in the centre of the serving plates.

Remove the tartar of salmon and crab from the forms and place in the centre of the cucumber circles, or serve in the ramekin dishes.

Garnish with salmon roe, lumpfish and sprigs of dill or a filled green olive or tomato.

The cucumber can be brushed with walnut oil to enhance the flavour.

CHEESE

Cheese is tops for taste and nourishment. Not only is it delicious, with a different type to suite every taste, it is also full of vitamins, protein and minerals, particularly calcium.

In the kitchen, cheese has traditionally been thought of as something to add to a dish to give it flavour, rather than as a complete meal in its own right. Today, however, more of us are valuing cheese as an excellent source of protein, not merely as a supplement to other ingredients. In fact, 1 lb (450 g) of cheese contains the same amount of protein as 1½ lb (675 g) of raw beef or fish or a dozen eggs.

The choice of cheeses available today is quite overwhelming. An incredible array confronts us when shopping - cheeses from home and from abroad, hard cheeses, semi-soft cheeses, soft cheeses, and low-fat ones. Since supermarkets have now replaced the more personalised family grocer, many of us have to rely on our own judgment when making a purchase.

Whenever possible, buy cheese freshly cut and remember that smaller pieces dry out quickly. If you do buy pre-packed pieces, avoid any that look too dry, too hard, too soft or "sweaty". Any cheeses that have cracks running along the edges or show a marked difference in colour between the centre and the edge are not fresh.

Although cheese often requires months to bring it to full maturity, once ripe it deteriorates comparatively rapidly. So it is best to buy only enough to last a few days to a week.

Always store cheese in a cool place - a larder is excellent - and cover lightly to protect but do not make the cover airtight. If left exposed, cheese will become hard and dry, but covered tightly it will tend to mould.

If mould does form on the surface, the cheese is not necessarily spoiled - the mould can be scraped off and the cheese used up quickly.

When cooking cheese, remember that too fierce a heat can make it stringy - it needs to melt rather than cook. Never let a sauce boil after adding cheese. Well-matured cheese with a high fat content is the ideal choice for cooking.

Glazed Goat's Cheese and Anchovies on Toast

Serves 4
CALORIES
Approximately 540 per portion

INGREDIENTS
11 oz/300 g goat's cheese without rind (St Maur or similar)
4 fl oz/100 ml dry white wine
1 clove garlic, peeled and crushed
1 tsp chopped herbs (basil, parsley, etc)
1 anchovy, finely chopped
pinch paprika powder
salt & freshly ground pepper
1 tbsp olive oil
French baguette
1 egg, lightly beaten

GARNISH
anchovy fillets
herbs of your choice

OVEN TEMPERATURE
240°C/475°F/Gas Mark 9

METHOD:

TOPPING
Pass the cheese through a sieve.

Add the white wine and stir until the mixture is smooth.

Add the garlic, herbs and anchovy.

Add the paprika, salt and pepper.

Keep aside.

TO FINISH OFF
Cut the baguette into slices. Sprinkle olive oil on the bread and spread the cheese mixture over the slices.

Brush with the egg.

Bake in the oven for about 3 minutes, until golden brown.

Remove and garnish with anchovies and herbs.

Serve immediately.

Feta Cheese Salad (left) & Glazed Goat's Cheese and Anchovies on Toast (right)

Feta Cheese Salad with a Herb and Caper Dressing

Serves 4

CALORIES
Approximately 430 per portion

INGREDIENTS
1 lb/450 g Feta cheese
1 clove garlic, peeled and crushed
1 tsp capers
1 red pepper, cut into strips
1 yellow pepper, cut into strips
2 tbsp herbs (basil, parsley, thyme, etc.)
4 fl oz/100 ml olive oil
juice of 1 lemon
salad leaves of your choice
salt & freshly ground pepper
8 black olives

METHOD
Cut the cheese into ¼ in/1 cm cubes.

Mix together the garlic, capers, peppers, herbs, olive oil and lemon juice. Season, pour over the cheese cubes and leave to marinate overnight.

TO FINISH OFF
Arrange the salad leaves on a plate.

Place the marinated Feta cheese cubes in the centre and garnish with olives and herbs.

SERVING CHEESE
To enjoy cheese at its best, never serve it direct from the refrigerator. The cold temperature will mask its flavour. Instead, always take it from the refrigerator at least 1 hour before eating and serve at room temperature.

OUTDOOR COOKING

Summer is the perfect time for barbecues: an easy and relaxed way to entertain friends. If you haven't barbecued before, give it a go. A few tries will help you to master the art of how to build the fire, control the heat and cook food to your taste.

There are so many products that you can use, particularly meat, such as chops, cutlets, sausages, steaks or kebabs. Chicken and duck joints or whole, small chickens are also suitable. Fish and shell fish need an experienced eye, as, although delicious barbecued, the delicate flesh quickly disintegrates over heat. Vegetables such as marinated courgettes or aubergines, large, flat mushrooms filled with herb and garlic butter, corn on the cob and potatoes wrapped in aluminium foil also make interesting accompaniments to a barbecue and are ideal for vegetarians.

Even dessert can be cooked over the fire. Try bananas grilled in their skins, or, better still, slit the skin open and insert a stick of lemon grass and a spoonful of honey. Peaches, peeled, halved and barbecued, are good too. Serve both with cream or vanilla ice-cream.

Barbecued Lamb Chops Marinated in Soya and Garden Herbs

Serves 2

CALORIES
Approximately 200 per portion

INGREDIENTS
6 small lamb chops, trimmed

MARINADE
4 tbsp vegetable oil
1 tbsp dark soya sauce
1 tsp grain mustard
1 clove garlic, crushed
¼ tsp fresh herbs, chopped - e.g. thyme, tarragon, chervil, rosemary (dried herbs can also be used)

METHOD
Mix together all the ingredients for the marinade. Place in a flat dish large enough to accommodate all the meat in one layer.

Add the lamb chops one by one, turning them in the marinade. Place them next to each other. Marinate for at least 30 minutes or preferably overnight.

TO FINISH OFF
Remove the chops from the marinade and season with salt.

Place on the barbecue on a hot spot and mark on both sides. Then move to the side and barbecue on a lower heat for about 5 minutes until medium cooked.

Rest for 2-3 minutes and serve with Barbecue Sauce (recipe on page 83).

Barbecued Prawns with Lemon Grass and Garlic

Serves 2

CALORIES
Approximately 60 per portion

INGREDIENTS
12 king prawns, peeled (thawed if frozen)
4 tbsp vegetable oil
2 cloves garlic, crushed
1 piece lemon grass, 1 in/2.5 cm long, cut in half lengthwise
2 cardamom seeds, crushed
¼ tsp coriander, chopped
salt & freshly ground pepper

METHOD
Heat the vegetable oil in a saucepan. Add the crushed garlic and lemon grass. Sweat on medium heat for about 2 minutes without colouring. Add the cardamom seeds. Add the coriander leaves and season with pepper. Remove from the heat and leave to cool. Add the prawns to the mixture and marinate overnight.

TO FINISH OFF
Remove from the marinade, season with salt and barbecue or grill.

Serve with half a lemon, or with sour cream flavoured with chopped dill and English mustard.

Barbecued Prawns with Lemon Grass and Garlic

Barbecue Sauce

Makes 125 ml (half a cup)

CALORIES
Approximately 50 per serving

INGREDIENTS
½ tbsp vegetable oil
¼ onion, finely chopped
1 clove garlic, finely chopped
3 tbsp tomato puree
¾ tbsp red wine vinegar
¼ pt/150 ml water
½ tbsp grain mustard
¼ tsp ground cinnamon
¼ tsp chilli, chopped (no seeds)

METHOD

Heat the oil, add the onion and garlic and sweat until transparent but without colouring.

Add the tomato puree and sweat for 2 minutes. Add the vinegar and water.

Add the grain mustard, gound cinnamon and chilli.

Cover and cook for about 20 minutes on a medium heat, stirring from time to time to make sure it does not stick.

Remove the lid and season with salt and pepper. Leave to cool. Refrigerate until ready for use.

MARINATE TO FLAVOUR

The trick to a really flavourful barbecue is to marinate your meat, fish, poultry or vegetables beforehand for at least 30 minutes, but for best results marinate overnight.
This enhances flavour and can help to tenderise by softening and moisturising the food. Never use salt in your marinade as this will bring out the water from the meat or fish. Also make sure that you don't place your food straight over the flame, as the dripping oil will catch fire and leave an unpleasant taste on the food.

Courgettes, or zucchini, are miniature marrows, from the same family as cucumber, squash and pumpkin They originate in the Mediterranean, but are now available here all year round. The height of their season, however, is from May to October when they make a particularly good buy.

When very young, and still bearing the flower petals, they are known as courgettes-fleur. These can be filled with a flavourful meat, fish or vegetable mixture, baked and served with a light sauce. However, mature courgettes are more widely available. These are about 6 inches (15 cm) long, and are usually straight and firm. Depending on the variety, they may be green, green and white striped or yellow. When buying, make sure that they are not too big, as they tend to become spongy. Always use within 3 days of purchase.

Courgettes are extremely versatile and can be used in many dishes, raw and cooked. Simply top and tail them, then cut into circles or slice lengthwise. Cook them simply in their own juice with herbs or combine them with peppers, onions and tomatoes for a ratatouille or stuff them with rice, meat or fish. Try them raw, added to your favourite salad, or tossed in vinaigrette or yoghurt dressing.

Gratinated Courgette and Bacon

Serves 2

CALORIES
Approximately 480 per portion

INGREDIENTS
11 oz/300 g potatoes, peeled and cut into ⅛ in/3 mm slices

1 shallot or ¼ onion, peeled and finely chopped

¼ clove garlic, peeled and finely chopped

7 fl oz/200 ml vegetable stock

1 tbsp vegetable oil

7 oz/200 g courgette, cut into strips

3 rashers bacon, cut into ½ in/1 cm strips

1 tsp each parsley, rosemary, chives (all chopped)

1 oz/25 g breadcrumbs, preferably brioche crumbs

salt & freshly ground pepper

2 tbsp Parmesan cheese, grated

OVEN TEMPERATURE
200°C/400°F/Gas Mark 6

METHOD
Place the potato slices, shallots and garlic in the vegetable stock and simmer for about 25-30 minutes on a low heat, covered with a lid. Season with salt and pepper. Place the potato mixture and cooking liquid in a greased oven-proof dish, filling it three quarters full. Leave to cool.

Brown the courgette strips on both sides in a non-stick pan using vegetable oil. Season with salt and pepper. Remove from the pan and place on top of the potatoes.

Place the bacon strips on an oven tray and grill them until crisp. Sprinkle on top of the courgettes.

Mix the breadcrumbs and chopped herbs and sprinkle this mixture on top of the courgettes and bacon.

Sprinkle the Parmesan cheese on top.

TO FINISH OFF
Place in a pre-heated oven for about 20 minutes until the top is golden brown.

BARBECUED COURGETTES

In the summer I love to barbecue. And what better way to treat a courgette?

Wash the courgettes, top and tail them, then slice in half lengthwise. Marinate for 1 hour in oil, crushed garlic and herbs. Then, just before they're required, pop them on a low fire for about 4-5 minutes on each side and season with salt and pepper. Quite delicious!

Gratinated Courgette and Bacon (top) & Courgette Soup with Almonds and Cinnamon (below)

Courgette Soup with Almonds and Cinnamon

Serves 4

CALORIES
Approximately 235 per portion

INGREDIENTS
2 oz/50 g almonds, flaked
1 oz/25 g unsalted butter
1 shallot or ¼ onion, peeled and finely chopped
½ clove garlic, peeled and finely chopped
¼ tsp mild curry powder
1 lb/450 g courgettes, sliced ⅛ in/3 mm thick
1¼ pt/750 ml chicken stock
5 fl oz/150 ml single cream
¼ tsp nutmeg
¼ tsp cinnamon

GARNISH
1 tbsp roasted almonds, sliced

METHOD
Boil the flaked almonds in salted water for 30 seconds. Drain and keep aside.

Melt the butter in a saucepan and sweat the shallots and garlic until transparent but without colouring. Add the curry powder and cook for 1 minute.

Add the sliced courgettes and sweat for 5 minutes, stirring constantly.

Add the boiled almonds and the chicken stock and simmer for 20 minutes.

Add the cream and boil for a further 5 minutes. Add the nutmeg and cinnamon. Season with salt and pepper. Use a blender to puree the soup, then pass through a sieve.

GARNISH
Roast the almonds under the grill on the highest heat until they are golden brown. Place in a kitchen towel and crush with your hands. Keep aside.

TO FINISH OFF
Bring the soup to the boil. Pour the soup into one large bowl or individual bowls. Sprinkle the roasted almonds on top, or serve separately.

DUCK

Whilst poultry is a great favourite in many of our homes, this generally means chicken or turkey. So for a special occasion, or just for a change, why not try duck? Duck is a great favourite in France, where Duck a l'Orange and Confit of Duck are often prepared for a family meal.

Duck is available all year round, both fresh and frozen, whole and portioned. Nowadays in this country most of the duck on sale comes from Lincolnshire and Norfolk. But the most famous, of course, are the Aylesbury ducks - named after the Buckinghamshire town from which they originate, although they are also bred elsewhere nowadays.

Fresh birds are at their best from August to December. When buying, make sure that you choose a bird with a plump breast and a pliable breast bone. Remember that a duck will feed fewer people than a chicken of the same weight. Allow about 1lb (450 g) dressed weight per person.

Duck is often thought of as a fatty bird. In fact, it is the skin that is full of fat, but as this gives the flesh its moistness and flavour, it should be left intact during cooking. Afterwards, it can be removed to provide a leaner meal, rich in protein and high in phosphorous and vitamins A and B.

Duck is traditionally roasted whole, with the classic accompaniment of a sage and onion stuffing and apple sauce. Allow 25-30 minutes cooking time per lb (450 g). Left-over roast duck makes a delicious addition to a summer salad. Alternatively, buy a whole duck, or joints, and try something deliciously different.

Roast Duck Breast with Sultana and Ginger Sauce

Serves 2

CALORIES
Approximately 800 calories per portion

INGREDIENTS
2 duck breasts
1 tbsp vegetable or sesame oil

SAUCE
1 tbsp sultanas
1 tsp butter
½ small shallot, peeled and chopped
4 fl oz/100 ml red wine
4 fl oz/100 ml Port wine
4 fl oz/100 ml chicken stock
½ tsp cornflour
1 tsp water
1 pinch ginger (fresh or powder)
salt & freshly ground white pepper

OVEN TEMPERATURE
170°C/325°F/Gas Mark 3

METHOD
Season the duck breasts. Heat the oil in a pan and place the breasts in it, skin side first. Bake in the oven for about 6 minutes, then turn and cook for a further 2 minutes. Remove from the pan and keep aside in a warm place.

SAUCE
Cook the sultanas in boiling water for 30 seconds. Refresh in cold water. Drain and keep aside.
Sweat the shallots in butter in a saucepan until transparent, but without colouring. Add the red wine and boil to half the quantity. Add port wine.
Add the chicken stock and boil to half the quantity. Pass through a sieve into a saucepan. Bring to the boil.
Dissolve the cornflour in cold water, add to the stock and cook for 2 minutes. Add the sultanas and ginger. Season.

TO FINISH OFF
Cut each duck breast at a slight angle into 3 pieces. Dress on a plate and pour 1-2 spoons of sauce on top. Serve the remaining sauce separately.

Duck Leg Casserole with Pineapple

Serves 4

CALORIES
Approximately 835 per portion

INGREDIENTS
1 tbsp vegetable oil
4 large duck legs
salt & freshly ground pepper

SAUCE
3 tbsp caster sugar
juice of 1 orange
7 fl oz/200 ml chicken stock
1 tbsp light soya sauce
3 tbsp ketchup
1 dash tabasco
2 tbsp white wine vinegar
1 tbsp cornflour
1 tbsp sherry
4 rings pineapple (canned in natural juice), drained and cut into ½ in/1 cm cubes

OVEN TEMPERATURE
180°C/350°F/Gas Mark 4

METHOD
Season the duck legs with salt and pepper.
Heat the oil in pan and fry the legs on both sides until golden brown.
Remove from the pan and keep aside.

SAUCE
Heat the sugar gently, without stirring, in a large saucepan on a medium heat, until it is golden brown.
Remove the pan from the heat and leave to cool for 2-3 minutes. Add the orange juice and hot chicken stock. Bring to the boil and simmer until the sugar has dissolved completely.
Add the soya sauce, ketchup and tabasco. Add the duck legs to the sauce and bring to the boil.
Simmer in the oven with a lid on for about 70-80 minutes until the duck legs are tender. To check that the duck legs are cooked, push a meat skewer into the thigh. If the juice that comes out is clear, they are cooked.

TO FINISH OFF
Remove the duck legs, place on a serving dish and keep warm.
Bring the sauce to the boil and add the vinegar. Dissolve the cornflour with the sherry and add to the sauce. Simmer for 3 minutes.
Pass through a sieve into a saucepan and skim off any fat with a spoon.
Bring to the boil and add the pineapple pieces. Season with salt and pepper.
Pour the sauce over the duck legs and serve.

ROASTING DUCK

When roasting a duck, always use a roasting rack in the oven tray.

This will allow the fat from the bird to drain away, leaving the skin to become crispy all over. Remember to baste the duck at regular intervals to ensure a crispy, succulent skin. If the bird is particularly fatty, the tray will need to be emptied during the cooking time.

SKATE

This curiously shaped fish, the skate or ray, lives close to the sea-bed in the open sea, or near the coast, where it is caught. There are several varieties of skate, some of which can grow to more that 10 feet (3 metres) long. Only the wing-shaped sides of the body and the breast fins are usable for culinary purposes, so skate are seldom seen whole in the fishmongers. Instead the fish is sold cut into "wings". They are in season from October to April.

Skate needs careful preparation. The skin should be washed well and scrubbed lightly before cooking. Alternatively buy the skate "wings" skinned, filleted and ready for use.

Most commonly fried in batter, skate is also delicious smoked, grilled or poached and served with a delicate sauce.

If you've not done so already, you'll discover that the thick, creamy flesh of skate is quite delicious.

Skate Wings with Basil and Caper Vinaigrette

Serves 2

CALORIES
Approximately 380 per portion

INGREDIENTS
2 small skate wings, 8 oz/225 g each

STOCK
½ bayleaf
3 peppercorns, crushed
1 small onion, sliced
8 fl oz/250 ml water
salt to taste

VINAIGRETTE
1 tbsp cooking stock, passed through a sieve (from above mixture)
2 tbsp white wine vinegar
1 shallot or ¼ onion, peeled and finely chopped
4 tbsp olive oil
1 medium tomato, peeled, deseeded and diced finely
1 tsp parsley, chopped
½ tsp basil, chopped
1 tsp capers, coarsely chopped
salt & freshly ground pepper

METHOD
Bring all the ingredients for the stock to the boil.

Add the skate wings, cover with a lid and simmer gently for about 20 minutes. Remove the skate wings and place on kitchen towel to absorb the cooking liquid.

VINAIGRETTE
Mix 1 tbsp of the cooking stock with the vinegar. Add the shallot or onion, olive oil, tomato, parsley, basil and capers. Season with salt and freshly ground pepper.

Keep aside.

TO FINISH OFF
Carefully place the skate wings on a serving dish.

Serve the vinaigrette separately or pour it over the fish.

Skate Wings with Leek and Butter Sauce

Serves 2

CALORIES
Approximately 470 per portion

INGREDIENTS
2 small skate wings, 8 oz/225 g each
chervil for garnish

STOCK
½ bay leaf
3 peppercorns, crushed
1 small onion, peeled and sliced
8 fl oz/250 ml water
salt to taste

BUTTER SAUCE
2 oz/50 g leek, white
1 shallot or ¼ onion, peeled and finely chopped
3 tbsp dry white wine
4 fl oz/100 ml cooking stock from above
3 oz/75 g cold butter, cut into ½ in/1 cm cubes
salt & freshly ground pepper

METHOD:

STOCK
Bring all the ingredients for the stock to the boil.

Add the skate wings, cover with a lid and simmer gently for about 20 minutes. Remove the skate wings and place on kitchen towel to absorb the cooking liquid.

BUTTER SAUCE
Cut the leek in half lengthwise and rinse under running water to remove any sand. Dry with a kitchen towel and cut into very small cubes. Cook in boiling salted water. Refresh in iced water, drain and keep aside.

Place the shallot, dry white wine and 4 fl oz/100 ml of the cooking stock in a saucepan. Bring to the boil and reduce the liquid until about 6 tbsp are left. Pass through a fine sieve into a saucepan. Bring to the boil and then remove from the heat.

Add the cubes of cold butter, stirring constantly and then add the leek cubes.

Reheat very gently on a low heat just to warm it up. Do not let it boil. Season with salt and pepper.

TO FINISH OFF
Pour the sauce onto 2 plates and place the skate wings on it. Garnish with chervil.

STORING FISH
If you buy fresh fish, try to use it on the day of purchase. If not, place it on a tray of ice cubes, cover with a cloth, then with clingfilm, and store in the fridge. This prevents other food from being affected by the odour of the fish.
Also bear in mind that whole fish should be gutted before storing and that they must not be stored for more than two days.

MUSSELS

Mussels are found growing naturally all over the world, including wild along our coasts. But most of the mussels available today are specially cultivated. Mussel farming, or myticulture, is done by planting stakes or hanging ropes in coastal waters. Mussels attach themselves and multiply on these. They are harvested at low tide and cleaned in tanks of purified water before going on sale.

In the shops they are available fresh, frozen raw or cooked and tinned in brine or smoked. Fresh mussels are at their best from September to March.

When buying mussels, allow 1½ pt/900 ml (about 12) per person as a main dish and ensure that they are alive until they are cooked. This means that they are closed, or will close immediately when lightly tapped and that they have a fresh sea smell. Discard any that remain open at this stage.

Preparation of fresh mussels is important. Firstly they must be scrubbed individually under running water and the "beards" removed. Then they should be rinsed twice in fresh water to ensure that all sand is removed. Discard any mussel that does not close tightly - one dead mussel could potentially cause food poisoning. Once cleaned, the mussels are ready for use. Any mussels that remain closed after being cooked must be discarded, as they are either dead or full of mud.

One of the most famous uses of mussels is the French dish, Moules Marinières. This, however, is not the only way in which they can be used. Try them freshly steamed in salad, with pasta, in a soup or added to a fish pie. They can also be gratinated, filled with garlic and herbs or chopped in a batter and fried as fritters.

Any way you choose will provide you with a nutritious dish, high in protein and a source of calcium and vitamin E too.

Basic Recipe for Cooking Mussels

Serves 2

CALORIES
Approximately 350 per portion

INGREDIENTS
3 pt/1.8 ltr (about 24) mussels

1 tbsp olive or vegetable oil

2 small shallots or ½ onion, peeled and finely chopped

1 clove garlic, peeled and finely chopped

4 fl oz/100 ml dry white wine

2 sprigs of thyme

freshly ground pepper

1 tsp herbs, chopped (your choice of parsley, dill or chervil)

juice of 1 lemon

2 oz/50 g butter, cut into small pieces

METHOD
Clean the mussels very carefully.

Heat the oil in a large pot. Add the shallots or onion and the garlic. Sweat until transparent, but without colouring. Add the mussels and thyme. Add the wine and season with pepper. Cover the pot with a lid and cook on high heat until the mussels are open. Remove from the heat.

Remove the mussels from the cooking liquid. Pass the cooking liquid through a muslin cloth into another saucepan. Bring to the boil and cook until you're left with one third of the original quantity of cooking liquid.

Remove the pan from the heat and add the chopped herbs. Whisk in the butter pieces and lemon juice. Pour over the mussels and serve.

STORING MUSSELS
Preferably use fresh mussels on the same day as they were purchased. If you have to store them overnight in the refrigerator, put them in a bowl with a plate on top, which is smaller than the bowl and weight it down slightly. This will prevent the mussels from opening and will retain the water inside.

Mussel and Noodle Salad

Serves 2

CALORIES
Approximately 460 per portion

INGREDIENTS
2 oz/50 g salad leaves (your choice of curly endive, mache, oak leaves, raddichio or any other leaves)

4 oz/100 g noodles (fresh)

1 tbsp vegetable oil

1½ pt/900 ml (about 12) fresh mussels

1 tbsp olive oil

½ small shallot, peeled and finely chopped

½ clove garlic, crushed

2 fl oz/50 ml white wine

freshly ground pepper

DRESSING
3 tbsp cold cooking stock from above (pass through a cloth)

pinch English mustard

juice of 1 lemon

2 tbsp olive or vegetable oil

1 tsp black olives, finely chopped

1 tsp dill and chervil

freshly ground white pepper

GARNISH
dill and sprigs of chervil

METHOD
Clean the salad leaves and keep aside.

Cook the noodles in boiling, salted water with the vegetable oil until cooked but still a little "crisp" inside. Refresh in cold water and drain. Keep aside.

Cook the mussels as described in the Basic Recipe for Cooking Mussels on page 92, using the olive oil, shallots, garlic and white wine. Remove the whole mussels from the shell and keep aside. Reduce the cooking liquid and reserve for the dressing.

DRESSING
Mix the cold cooking liquid with the mustard. Add the lemon juice, olive oil, chopped olives and herbs. Season to taste and keep aside.

TO FINISH OFF
Arrange the salad leaves and noodles on 2 plates. Place the mussels on top. Spoon the dressing over the salad. Garnish with dill and chervil.

PEACHES

The peach is one of the finest fruits. In fact, it is hard to beat a ripe peach, with its velvety skin and juicy flesh.

Peaches originate from China, but are now widely grown around the world. This means that they are in the shops almost all year round - peaking between July and September.

There are basically two types of the fruit available: cling stone peaches, which have a firm flesh and are particularly good for bottling, and free stone peaches, which are mainly eaten fresh.

In addition to these, there is the delicious nectarine. Contrary to popular belief, this is not a cross between a peach and a plum, but a true variant of the peach and it can be treated in exactly the same way. The main difference between the two fruits is the skin. The skin of peaches is furry, while nectarines are completely smooth and their colouring is generally more vivid.

Look out for firm fruit and avoid any that are split, bruised or browning. Allow the fruit to ripen at room temperature but only buy enough to last for a few days, as it does not keep well.

The skin of a ripe fruit will peel off easily and the stone virtually rattles around inside. Flesh will vary from bright yellow to greenish-white, depending on the variety.

Peaches prove the point that being delicious does not necessarily mean being high in calories too. An average fruit contains about 40 calories and is also high in fibre and vitamins A and C.

Peaches and nectarines are extremely versatile. Naturally, they are delicious eaten fresh or in a fruit salad. But they can also be used in many hot or cold dishes - sweet and savoury - and they are popular as a juice, dried, preserved in syrup or brandy, or made into jam or chutney. They are also good grilled on the barbecue.

Fresh Peach Compote with Vanilla and Cinnamon

Serves 4

CALORIES
Approximately 310 per portion

INGREDIENTS
6 large firm peaches
7 oz/200 g caster sugar
8 fl oz/250 ml fresh orange juice
1 tsp lemon rind
1 pinch cinnamon powder
vanilla pod cut in half lengthwise
1 tbsp Grand Marnier or orange or peach liqueur
mint to garnish

OPTIONAL
vanilla ice cream
mint or berries

METHOD

Peel the peaches. Cut the fruit into quarters, then remove and discard the stones and place the peach pieces in a bowl. Mix together the sugar, orange juice, lemon rind, cinnamon and the vanilla pod in a saucepan.

Heat gently, without stirring, until the sugar is dissolved, then bring to the boil.

Pour the hot liquid over the peach pieces and cover with a lid.

Leave to cool.

Then carefully drain the syrup from the fruits into a saucepan. Bring the syrup to the boil and simmer until it is reduced to half the quantity.

Add the Grand Marnier or orange or peach liqueur. Pour the hot syrup over the peaches.

Leave to cool.

Garnish with mint or fresh berries and serve with vanilla ice-cream or fresh cream.

TO SKIN A PEACH
Most recipes using peaches require the skin to be removed. Make light work of this - use only ripe fruits and simply place the peaches in boiling water for 10 seconds, then refresh in iced water and peel. The skin will slide off.

Fresh Peach Compote with Vanilla and Cinnamon (top) & Peach and Mascarpone Cheese Mousse (below)

Peach and Mascarpone Cheese Mousse

Serves 4

CALORIES
Approximately 290 per portion

INGREDIENTS
6 ripe peaches, yellow or white

MOUSSE
¼ tsp lemon rind

1 tbsp lemon juice

¼ tsp vanilla essence

4½ tbsp caster sugar

2 tbsp white rum

4 oz/100 g Mascarpone cheese

4 fl oz/100 ml double cream, whipped

3 level tsp gelatine powder

GARNISH (OPTIONAL)
1 peach

mint leaves

METHOD
Peel the peaches. Remove the stones from 2 of the peaches and cut the fruit into ½ in/1 cm cubes. Keep these aside.

Cut the remaining 4 peaches into quarters and remove the stones.

Mix together the lemon rind, lemon juice, vanilla essence and the sugar with the peach quarters. Then puree the fruit and place in a saucepan. Heat on top of the stove until hot but not boiling. Remove from the heat and immediately sprinkle over the gelatine powder. Stir in until dissolved and then add the rum.

Leave to cool, then mix in the Mascarpone cheese. Fold in the whipped cream using a wooden spoon.

TO FINISH OFF
Divide the cubed peaches into 4 portions and place in the bottom of 4 glasses or in a bowl. Pour the Mascarpone cheese mixture on top. Leave to cool for about 4 hours in the refrigerator. Garnish with mint or a small fan of fresh peach.

Although tea was brought to Britain in the middle of the 17th century, it was not until much later that it became widely available and was enjoyed for breakfast or after dinner.

The long gap between lunch and dinner encouraged people to take tea between the main meals. This became most popular with those who could afford this luxury and fashionable society took tea at about 4 pm. At this time, afternoon tea was served with very thinly sliced bread and butter, Dundee cake and toasted muffins.

Later, afternoon tea was served at a later hour and became a meal in itself. Chicken cutlets, oysters and other savouries were offered to accompany the sandwiches, bread and cake. Sometimes musicians would perform to turn it into a full social event.

Today few of us have time to enjoy such occasions mid-afternoon. Even so, afternoon tea has never lost its symbolic position as a British tradition, and, for a special treat, how better to enjoy oneself than over a steaming cup of tea and a slice of cake, a tart or a delicate sandwich.

Almond Tartlets

Makes about 12 tartlets

CALORIES
Approximately 500 per tartlet

INGREDIENTS:
SWEET PASTRY
4 oz/100 g caster sugar
9 oz/200 g butter, cold, and cut into small cubes
1 egg, lightly whisked
12 oz/350 g soft plain flour

FILLING
4 oz/100 g caster sugar
4 oz/100 g unsalted butter, at room temperature
2 eggs, lightly whisked
3 oz/75 g ground almonds
1 oz/25 g plain flour
4 drops almond essence
2 oz/50 g red jam
12 almonds
2 oz/50 g apricot jam (clear)

OVEN TEMPERATURE
180°C/350°F/Gas Mark 4

METHOD:

SWEET PASTRY
Mix together the sugar and butter until they are just bound together. Mix in the egg. Mix in the flour. Do not over work. Leave in the refrigerator for 1 hour.

FILLING
Whisk together the sugar and butter until light and fluffy. Gradually add the eggs.
Very gently mix in the almonds, flour and almond essence. Do not overmix, otherwise the mixture will split.

TO FINISH OFF
Roll out the pastry to ⅛ in/3 mm thick. Cut out round shapes and line small cases which are 3 in/6 cm in diameter. Put ½ tsp of red jam in each case.
Spoon or pipe the filling equally between the cases on top of the red jam. Place an almond on top of each tartlet as a garnish.
Bake in the oven for about 20 minutes or until cooked and golden brown.
Leave to cool and brush with boiled clear apricot jam. If you are using jam with pieces of fruit in it, remove the pieces by passing the jam through a sieve.

SANDWICH FILLINGS
Try the following ideas as alternatives to the traditional sandwich fillings:
* Thinly sliced black pudding fried crisply, skin removed and coarsely chopped, then bound together with some mayonnaise and spring onions.
* Flaked smoked trout with creme fraiche, horseradish and chopped dill.
* Cottage cheese with sliced roast chicken and chives.
* Strips of roast duck meat mixed with plum sauce, mayonnaise, cucumber and spring onions.
* Grill some vegetables and marinate them in olive oil and herbs and serve on pieces of French stick and as a special treat, top with mozzarella cheese.

Linzertorte

Makes 2 tarts

CALORIES
Approximately 350 per portion

INGREDIENTS
4 oz/125 g caster sugar
8 oz/225 g unsalted butter, cold, and cut into cubes
1 egg
1 egg yolk
13 oz/375 g plain flour
4 oz/125 g ground hazelnuts
½ tsp ground cloves
½ tsp ground cinnamon
1 drop lemon essence
1 egg, mixed with 2 tbsp milk for egg wash
4 oz/100 g raspberry jam

OVEN TEMPERATURE
180°C/350°F/Gas Mark 4

METHOD

Mix together the sugar and butter until they are bound together. Gradually add the whole egg and the egg yolk. Mix in the flour, ground hazelnuts, clove, cinnamon and lemon essence.

Knead to a dough and leave in the refrigerator for about 45 minutes. Line 2 flan rings, 8 in/20 cm in diameter, with greaseproof paper. Roll out the dough to ¼ in/4 mm thick. Cut 2 circles 8 in/20 cm in diameter and place in the flan rings. Spread the jam on the base of the circles, leaving ¼ in/5 mm around the edges. Roll out the remaining pastry to ¼ in/5 mm thick and cut into strips ½ in/1 cm wide. Use these strips to create a lattice pattern on the tarts.

Then cut 2 strips ¾ in/1.5 cm wide. Brush with egg wash and place the strips inside the flan rings to form a border around the edges of the tarts. Egg wash lightly and mark the edges with a fork.

Bake in the oven for 25 minutes. Remove from the oven, leave to cool and serve.

PEARS

There are over 3,000 varieties of pears, each with their own characteristics, but only a few of them are grown commercially. The best known in this country are the Conference (September-June), the Comice (October-March) and the Williams (September-October). Many other varieties are imported.

Pears, like apples, are divided into two categories: dessert and cooking varieties. Conference, Comice and Williams are dessert pears which are usually eaten fresh, but are also deli-cious poached, stewed or used for other culinary purposes.

Cooking pears, such as the Duchess, however, have tougher flesh, which makes them unsuitable for fresh eating but ideal for cooking.

Like most fruit, pears make a nutritious contribution to any meal, especially when eaten whole with the skin on.

An average pear provides only 40 calories, but is high in fibre and rich in vitamins A and C.

Gammon Steak with Pear and Potato Salad

Serves 4

CALORIES
Approximately 400 per portion

INGREDIENTS
1 ripe pear
1 lb/450 g potato
4 gammon steaks

DRESSING
2 fl oz/50 ml white wine vinegar
1 tbsp mild mustard
1 tbsp vegetable oil
½ onion, peeled and finely chopped
5 fl oz/150 ml vegetable stock
2 tsp chives, chopped

GARNISH (OPTIONAL)
mixed salad leaves
chervil

METHOD

Peel the pear and cut into quarters. Remove the core and pips. Cook in boiling water for about 8 minutes. Leave to cool. Remove from the cooking liquid and cut into ¼ in/5 mm slices. Keep aside.

Cook the potatoes in their skins and peel while still warm. Cut into ¼ in/5mm thick slices

DRESSING

Mix the vinegar and mustard. Keep aside.

Heat the vegetable oil and sweat the onions until transparent but without colouring. Add the vegetable stock and boil for 2 minutes.

Remove from the heat and add the vinegar and mustard mixture.

Season with salt and pepper.

Mix together the potato and pear slices and pour the warm dressing over the mixture.

Leave to rest for about 30 minutes. Add the chopped chives.

TO FINISH OFF

Grill the gammon steaks.

Arrange the salad in the centre of the plates with the salad leaves around.

Place the gammon steaks on top and garnish with chervil. Serve.

RIPENING PEARS

All pears bruise easily, so handle with care. They are best bought slightly under-ripe and left to ripen in a warm place. Once ready, move to somewhere cool, as they deteriorate quickly.

Gammon Steak with Pear and Potato Salad

Pear and Blackcurrant Pancakes

Serves 4 (about 2 pancakes each)

CALORIES
Approximately 370 per portion

INGREDIENTS
1½ oz/40 g flour
5 fl oz/150 ml milk
1 egg, size 3
½ tsp oil
butter to grease the pan

FILLING
3 pears
1 oz/25 g butter
juice of 1 orange
4 fl oz/100 ml white wine
1 tbsp caster sugar
cinnamon to taste
5 oz/150 g blackcurrants
icing sugar

METHOD:

PANCAKES

Place the flour in a mixing bowl. Blend in the milk, beaten egg and oil. Cover the bowl and leave to rest for 10 minutes.

Brush a non-stick pan with melted butter, add 2 tbsp of the batter and swirl the pan to coat evenly. Cook the pancake until the underside is golden. Turn and cook until both sides are golden. Make 8 pancakes in this way, using up all the batter. Remove from the pan and keep aside. Do not lay the pancakes on top of each other as they will stick.

FILLING

Peel the pears and cut into 4 pieces lengthwise. Cut into ¼ in/5 mm pieces. Heat the butter and sweat the pear pieces for about 1 minute without them colouring. Add the orange juice, wine, caster sugar and cinnamon. Bring to the boil and cook until the pear pieces are tender.
Drain the liquid through a sieve into a pan and keep the pears aside.
Bring the liquid to the boil and cook until half the quantity is left. Add the blackcurrants and bring to the boil.
Mix with the pears that were kept aside.

TO FINISH OFF

Place the pancakes in front of you and divide the filling equally into the centre of each pancake. Fold one side over the other to form a half-moon shape. Place in an ovenproof dish and sprinkle with icing sugar. Place under the grill to brown. Serve with cream.

APPLES

A is for apples - probably the most popular fruit of all! They are freely available all year round, inexpensive, extremely versatile and, of course, good to eat.

Apples are divided into two categories: dessert or eating apples and cooking apples. While dessert apples are not only good for eating, but are also good for cooking with too, cooking apples are best reserved for culinary purposes only.

Dessert apples are available all year round - imports ensure a plentiful supply - but in autumn lots of home-grown varieties are on sale.

Cooking apples are mainly home-grown and are available from late summer through the winter. Whatever type you are buying, make sure you choose fruits that are firm, with smooth skin and no blemishes.

If stored in a cool place, apples will keep for a couple of weeks, making them a useful standby to have on hand.

Naturally a crunchy apple makes a delicious, healthy snack at any time, but apples have many other uses.

Try them stewed, as a compote or sauce, combined with carrots for a healthy salad or as a garnish with poultry or game.

With a warm apple pie or moist apple cake, you are certain to have requests for second helpings every time!

Apple and Ginger Cake

Makes about 8 slices

CALORIES
Approximately 390 per slice

INGREDIENTS
3 oz/75 g sultanas
2 tbsp brandy
8 oz/250 g self-raising flour
1 tsp salt
4 oz/125 g butter
4 oz/125 g caster sugar
1 tsp ginger
½ tsp cinnamon
1 lb/450 g apples
2 eggs, size 3, lightly beaten
icing sugar to garnish

OVEN TEMPERATURE
200°C/400°F/Gas Mark 6

METHOD

Line and grease a cake tin, 7 in/18 cm in diameter, with greaseproof paper. Dust with flour and keep aside.

Soak the sultanas in the brandy and keep aside.

Mix the flour with the salt. Rub the butter into the flour. Add the sugar, ginger and cinnamon. Keep aside.

Peel the apples. Cut into quarters, remove the core and pips. Slice the apple quarters crosswise into ⅛ in/3 mm pieces and add these to the mixture. Add the soaked sultanas. Add the lightly beaten eggs and mix thoroughly.

Spoon the mixture evenly into the prepared tin. Bake for 30-40 minutes in the oven.

Use a knife to check if the cake is cooked inside. Remove from the oven.

To FINISH OFF

Leave the cake to rest for about 10 minutes, then remove from the tin.

Sprinkle the edges of the cake with icing sugar and serve either with hot Fresh Apple Sauce (recipe on page 101) or with vanilla or cinnamon ice cream.

TO TEST A CAKE

The simplest method to test a cake is to insert a metal skewer (or slim knife) into the centre. If the skewer comes out clean, the cake will be cooked to perfection. If not, return the cake to the oven and re-test later.
With the Apple and Ginger Cake above, the skewer will look quite moist due to the high volume of apples - but the cake batter must, of course, be cooked through.

Apple and Ginger Cake

Fresh Apple Sauce

Serves 4

CALORIES
Approximately 180 per portion

INGREDIENTS
2 apples

1 oz/25 g butter

4 fl oz/100 ml white wine

1 piece lemon grass, 1 in/2.5 cm (optional)

pinch cinnamon

1 oz/25 g caster sugar

4 fl oz/100 ml single cream

brandy to taste (optional)

METHOD

Peel the apples and cut into quarters. Remove the core and pips with a knife.

Cut into small pieces about 1 in/2.5 cm square.

Heat the butter in a pan. Add the apple pieces and sweat for 1 minute, without colouring.

Add the white wine, cinnamon and lemon grass and cover with a lid. Cook on a medium heat until soft. Add the sugar and cream and bring to the boil. Remove the lemon grass.

Puree the mixture in a food mixer, then return to pan and bring back to the boil. Add brandy, if desired, and serve hot.

COD

Cod are large, deep-sea fish, which are available all year round, but at their best during the summer months. They have long been recognised for their versatility - the delicate, creamy flesh lends itself well to many ways of preparation.

Cod can be bought whole, in fillets or in steaks. When buying, look for a whole fish with a bright sheen, red gills and flesh that springs back when prodded. If buying portions, avoid flesh that looks limp or dry, as this indicates that it is past its best.

Cod is available not only fresh and frozen, but also smoked and salted. Smoked fillets should not be confused with smoked haddock, but can be treated in much the same way, whilst salted cod - "Morue" - is particularly popular on the continent and should be soaked before using.

And, of course, in addition to the flesh, cod roe is available too, sold either uncooked, boiled or smoked. Even the tongues are considered a delicacy by some. And last but not least, the liver is used in the manufacture of cod liver oil.

A truly versatile fish!

Cod Fishcake with Coriander and Tomato

Serves 4

CALORIES
Approximately 250 per portion

INGREDIENTS
8 oz/200 g potato

1 lb/450 g cod fillet, no skin or bones

1 shallot or ¼ onion, peeled and finely chopped

1 egg, lightly beaten

1 tsp parsley, chopped

pinch chilli powder

salt & freshly ground pepper

3 tbsp vegetable oil

flour to dust the fishcakes

CORIANDER AND TOMATO SAUCE

1 tbsp vegetable oil

1 shallot or ¼ onion, finely chopped

1 clove garlic, peeled and crushed

¼ tsp red chilli, deseeded and finely chopped

¼ tsp tomato puree

4 fl oz/100 ml white wine

4 tomatoes, peeled, deseeded and coarsely chopped

1 tsp coriander, finely chopped

salt & freshly ground pepper

OVEN TEMPERATURE
180°C/350°F/Gas Mark 4

METHOD:

CAKES
Cook the potato in its skin. Peel, mash lightly with a fork and keep aside.
Season the cod and place on a greased oven tray. Bake in the oven until cooked, then flake the fish while it is still warm.
Mix together the fish, shallot or onion, potatoes and egg. Add the chopped parsley and chilli powder and season with salt and pepper.
Divide the mixture into 8 equal portions and form into round cakes 1 in/2.5 cm thick. Place on greaseproof paper and keep aside.

SAUCE
Heat the oil in a saucepan. Add the shallot or onion and the garlic. Sweat until transparent but without colouring. Add the chillis. Add the tomato puree and cook for 2 minutes, stirring continuously. Add the wine. Add the tomato and cook for 5 minutes. Season with salt and pepper.
Remove from the heat and add the coriander leaves.

TO FINISH OFF
Heat the oil in a non-stick pan. Dust the fishcakes with flour and fry gently on both sides until golden brown.
Arrange on a plate and serve the sauce separately.

PREPARING COD
Cod is often accused of being watery. To avoid this, always prepare fresh cod in the following way before following your chosen recipe:

- Wash the flesh and dry well
- Sprinkle lightly with salt
- Cover and refrigerate for about 1 hour
- Dry thoroughly before using

Cod with Anchovies and Courgettes

Serves 2

CALORIES
Approximately 360 per portion

INGREDIENTS
1 egg

2 cod steaks, each about 7 oz/200 g

flour to dust fish

VEGETABLES

2 tbsp olive or vegetable oil

1 shallot or ¼ onion, peeled and finely chopped

1 clove garlic, peeled and crushed

4 fl oz/100 ml white wine

4 fl oz/100 ml fish stock

9 oz/250 g courgettes, ends cut off and diced

3 anchovies, coarsely chopped

1 tomato, medium size, peeled, deseeded and diced

½ tsp basil, chopped

½ tsp parsley, chopped

salt & freshly ground white pepper

GARNISH

fresh herbs

OVEN TEMPERATURE

170°C/325°F/Gas Mark 3

METHOD
Whisk the egg lightly with a fork. Season the cod with salt and pepper. Dust with flour on both sides. Dip the cod in the beaten egg mixture. Heat the oil in a non-stick pan. Pan-fry the cod steak until golden brown on both sides. Remove from the pan and place in an oven-proof dish. Bake in the oven for 7-8 minutes until cooked.

VEGETABLES
Heat the oil in a saucepan. Add the shallot or onion and garlic and sweat until transparent but without colouring. Add the wine and fish stock and boil until about 6 tbsp of the liquid is left. Add the courgettes and cook - they should be slightly crisp. Add the anchovies and tomato and bring to the boil. Season and add the chopped herbs.

TO FINISH OFF
Place the vegetables on a dish and the cod in the centre.
Garnish with fresh herbs.

PUMPKIN

The pumpkin is a member of the squash family, closely related to the marrow. In this country they are less commonly used than in America, where, in autumn, one can find a wide variety on sale and where they are used in many different ways ... including being turned into wicked lanterns for "Trick or Treaters"!

American pumpkins can weigh up to 100 lb (45 kg), but those found here tend to be much smaller. They are available whole, or, on occasion, they are sold by the piece. If buying a whole pumpkin, choose a medium-sized one, or, if cut, one that has smooth, non-stringy flesh.

As the Americans have found, pumpkins make a delicious addition to many different dishes, both savoury and sweet. One of my favourite methods of cooking pumpkin is roast-ing: simply peel, remove the seeds and cut the flesh into wedges. Then roast the pieces around a joint, like potatoes.

Alternatively, pumpkins can be baked, steamed, boiled or mashed, used in salads, or for compote or sweet pickles.

Pumpkin is also delicious served with a cheese sauce, added to a meat pie or mixed with other vegetables in a cream soup. Allow 8 oz (200 g) per person when using as a vegetable.

Alternatively, give pumpkin the sweet treatment. If you have not done so before, try a pumpkin pie - sweet and spicy, it makes a delicious autumn dessert. You can also give your apple pie a boost by adding pumpkin with cinnamon to flavour.

Pumpkin and Dried Apricot Cake (left) & Pumpkin Muffins (right)

Pumpkin and Dried Apricot Cake

Makes about 8 slices

CALORIES
Approximately 420 per slice

INGREDIENTS
11 oz/300 g pumpkin, peeled and roughly chopped
7 oz/200 g dried apricots, roughly chopped
2 tbsp brandy
9 oz/250 g unsalted butter, room temperature
6 oz/175 g caster sugar
2 eggs, size 3, lightly beaten
2 oz/50 g desiccated coconut
12 oz/325 g self-raising flour
4 fl oz/125 ml milk
pinch of salt
icing sugar to garnish

OVEN TEMPERATURE
170°C/325°F/Gas Mark 3

METHOD

Line the bottom of a round cake tin, 9 in/24 cm in diameter (or a rectangular tin of equivalent size), with greaseproof paper. Grease the sides of the tin.

Cook the pumpkin in boiling water until tender. Drain, mash and leave to cool. Keep aside.

Soak the apricots in the brandy. Keep aside.

Mix the butter and sugar until smooth and creamy. Add the coconut and the eggs. Add a little milk and self-raising flour alternately to the mixture and mix until smooth. Add a pinch of salt, the apricots and pumpkin.

Spoon the mixture into the tin and bake for about 1 hour, or until cooked.

Remove from the oven and leave to rest for 15 minutes before removing from the tin. Cool on a cooling rack. Sprinkle icing sugar on top.

Alternatively this can be served as a dessert, slightly warm with honey ice-cream.

Pumpkin Muffins

Makes about 10-12 muffins

CALORIES
Approximately 290 per muffin

INGREDIENTS
8 oz/225 g pumpkin
6 oz/175 g butter, room temperature
6 oz/175 g Demerara sugar
3 eggs, size 3
9 oz/250 g wholemeal flour
3 tsp baking powder
6 tsp mixed spice
½ tsp salt
3 fl oz/75 ml milk
3 oz/75 g sultanas

OVEN TEMPERATURE
200°C/400°F/Gas Mark 6

METHOD

Line muffin or cup cake tins with paper cases.

Cook the pumpkin in boiling water until it is tender. Drain, mash and leave to cool. Keep aside.

Mix together the sugar and butter until smooth and creamy. Add the eggs and milk gradually using a wooden spoon.

Sieve together the flour and baking powder. Add to the mixture together with the mixed spices and salt. Mix until the mixture is smooth. Add the sultanas and pumpkin.

Spoon the mixture into the paper cases and bake in the oven for approximately 25 minutes until cooked.

Serve warm with butter.

FLAVOURFUL PUMPKINS

Pumpkins are often accused of being watery and lacking in flavour.
For the fullest flavour they need to be well dried before use. When you've picked or bought your pumpkin, store it whole in a cool, dry place for up to 1 month.
Once cut, a pumpkin must be stored in the fridge and eaten within a week.
It can also be frozen raw or cooked for future use.

PASTA

Pasta has rapidly gained in popularity in this country over recent years. Nowadays not only is it available dried, ready to cook, but many shops also stock a whole range of fresh pasta. It is not only delicious and versatile, but also quick and easy to use.

Pasta is literally a "paste" made from Amber durum wheat and water. Egg is sometimes added to give a richer flavour. The paste is then thinly rolled or extruded through a special machine and formed into shapes, sometimes enclosing fillings.

Olives are added to make black noodles, spinach to make green or tomato to make pink, or other flavours are used, such as basil, poppy seed, roasted hazelnut, saffron - the list is endless. For those wanting to add fibre to their diet, there is also a wholewheat variety of pasta.

All pasta is boiled and cooking time varies according to shape, size and freshness. Allow 2 oz (50 g) per person as a side dish or double this for a main dish. Pasta is not laden with calories. Fresh pasta contains approximately 160 calories per 2 oz/50 g. For those watching their weight, it's the sauces that need attention!

Pasta can be served as a savoury main dish, as a side dish, instead of potatoes or rice, as a starter or as a garnish with soup. It is delicious served with butter or a savoury sauce. Traditionally it is accompanied by grated Parmesan cheese.

Pasta with Anchovies and Peppers

Serves 4

CALORIES
Approximately 410 per portion

INGREDIENTS
1 lb/450 g fresh pasta
2 tbsp vegetable oil

SAUCE
2 tbsp vegetable oil
1 small onion or 3 shallots, peeled and finely chopped
1 clove garlic, finely chopped
7 oz/200 g courgette, diced
7 oz/200 g peppers, red or yellow, seeds removed and diced
1 tsp tomato puree
2 large tomatoes, peeled, deseeded and diced
4 fl oz/100 ml vegetable stock
4 anchovy fillets, finely chopped
salt & freshly ground pepper
½ tsp basil, chopped

METHOD:

SAUCE
Sweat the onion or shallot and the garlic in oil until transparent but without colouring.

Add the courgette and peppers and sweat for a further minute. Add the tomato puree and sweat for one more minute, stirring constantly. Add the diced tomato and vegetable stock and bring to the boil. Reduce the heat and simmer on a low heat for about 15 minutes until the peppers are cooked.

Add anchovies, season with salt and pepper and remove from the heat.

TO FINISH OFF
Cook the pasta in boiling salted water and vegetable oil until cooked "al dente".

Drain and season with salt and pepper. Arrange on warm plates.

Reheat the sauce, add the chopped basil and spoon over the pasta.

COOKING PASTA
To cook pasta, use a large pot - if possible you should have 10 times more water than pasta. Always add some oil to the water, as this will prevent the pasta from sticking together. Pasta should be cooked "al dente" - that is, it should have a "bite" and not be overcooked and too soft.

Pasta in Tuna and Stilton Sauce

Serves 4

CALORIES
Approximately 660 per portion

INGREDIENTS
1 lb/450 g fresh pasta
1 tbsp vegetable oil for cooking

SAUCE
1½ tbsp vegetable oil
½ small onion or 2 shallots, peeled and finely chopped
2 fl oz/50 ml dry sherry
2 fl oz/50 ml fish stock
14 fl oz/400 ml single cream
1 tbsp Stilton cheese, passed through a sieve
4 oz/100 g tinned tuna, drained and flaked
1 tsp dill, chopped (fresh or dried)
sprig of dill for garnish
salt & freshly ground white pepper

METHOD:

SAUCE
Heat the oil in a saucepan and sweat the onion or shallot until transparent but without colouring.

Add the sherry and stock and bring to the boil. Add the cream and boil for about 6-7 minutes, stirring until it is creamy.

Whisk in the Stilton. Bring the sauce quickly to the boil. Add the tuna fish.

Remove from the heat. Add the chopped dill. Season with salt and pepper.

TO FINISH OFF
Cook the pasta in boiling salted water and vegetable oil until "al dente". Drain and keep aside.

Mix the sauce and pasta in a warm dish. Garnish with a sprig of dill and serve.

POTATOES

We consume more potatoes in Britain than any other European country, yet it was only during the relatively recent Industrial Revolution that the potato caught on here. Prior to this the potato enjoyed an exotic history: first cultivated by the Incas in South America, they were later adopted by the Spanish, then the French and finally introduced as a novelty to the court of Queen Elizabeth I by Sir Walter Raleigh!

With more than 200 recognised varieties available, the potato is valued as a versatile and nutritious addition to our cuisine. Both main crop and early potatoes are on sale throughout the year, with home-grown varieties available from May. Early potatoes should be purchased in small quantities, as they quickly lose their crisp flavour, while main crop potatoes have better keeping qualities. All potatoes bruise easily, so they should be treated with care and stored loose in a cool, airy, dark place.

The potato has become one of our staple foods. It is low in fat, has no cholesterol and is a good source of Vitamin C, essential minerals and fibre. Contrary to popular belief, it is also low in calories. However, beware of many popular cooking methods which are often calorie-laden.

In our busy lives it is all too easy to get stuck in a rut, using the same old methods of preparation time and time again. The potato lends itself to so many ways of cooking: all that is needed is a little time and curiosity and you'll be surprised by what you can achieve with the potato!

Jacket Potatoes Filled with Ginger Prawns

Serves 2

CALORIES
Approximately 425 per portion

INGREDIENTS
1 large baking potato
1 egg yolk

FILLING
1 oz/25 g butter
1 oz/25 g onion or shallot, peeled and finely chopped
4 oz/100 g peeled prawns, fresh or frozen
2 fl oz/50 ml white wine
5 fl oz/150 ml single cream
pinch ground ginger
salt & freshly ground pepper
dill and parsley, chopped

OVEN TEMPERATURE
180°C/350°F/Gas Mark 4

METHOD
Make a small incision in the potato and bake in the oven for about 1 hour depending on size. Remove from the oven, rest for 10 minutes then cut in half lengthwise. Hollow out the centre of each half of the potato with a spoon until about one third of the potato is left on the skin. Mash the loose potato in a bowl and season with salt and freshly ground pepper. Mix in the egg yolk and keep aside.

FILLING

Melt the butter in a saucepan, add the onion or shallot and sweat until transparent. Add the prawns and sweat for 30 seconds. Add the ginger. Remove from the pan and keep aside. Using the same pan, boil the wine until half the quantity remains. Add the cream and boil until half the quantity remains and a thick, creamy consistency is obtained. Add the prawns. Season. Remove from the heat and allow to cool. Add the chopped dill and parsley.

TO FINISH OFF
Season the potato shells then spoon in the prawn and cream filling, being careful not to overfill. Using a piping bag pipe the potato mixture to cover the top of each potato basket being careful not to overfill.

Bake in the oven on a tray for about 15 minutes until hot and golden brown.

PEELING POTATOES

When using potatoes, remember that many of the nutrients are in, or just under, the skin. For this reason, whenever possible use the potato unpeeled or, if you must peel it, peel very thinly. Again, to preserve their nutritional value, prepare when required and avoid leaving them to soak in water.

Leek and Potato Gratin

Serves 4

CALORIES
Approximately 330 per portion

INGREDIENTS
4 oz/100 g medium size leeks, not too green
1 oz/25 g butter or margarine
½ clove garlic, peeled and finely chopped
2 fl oz/50 ml dry white wine
10 fl oz/300 ml single cream
1 lb/450 g potato
2 tbsp grated cheese (Parmesan if possible)
salt & freshly ground white pepper
grated nutmeg

OVEN TEMPERATURE
190°C/375°F/Gas Mark 5

METHOD

Remove the stalk and dark-green leaves of the leek. Cut the leek in half lengthwise, then in half again lengthwise. Cut each piece crosswise into ½ in/1 cm pieces. Wash thoroughly to remove any sand. Drain and dry with kitchen towel.

Heat the butter or margarine in a saucepan. Sweat the leek and garlic for 1 minute without colouring. Add the wine, bring to the boil and cover with a lid.

Simmer on low heat for 4-5 minutes. Add the cream, bring back to the boil and remove from the heat.

Peel the potatoes, cut into ⅛ in/3 mm slices and add to the leek and cream mixture. Bring to the boil and season with salt, pepper and nutmeg. Pour the mixture into an ovenproof dish and sprinkle with cheese.

TO FINISH OFF

Bake in the oven for about 20-25 minutes until cooked and golden brown. If necessary, pop under the grill to brown. Serve immediately.

BERRIES

Summer time is berry time, with some types being available through to September. Blueberries, blackberries, blackcurrants, raspberries, loganberries, strawberries, redcurrants and gooseberries are all in plentiful supply during the summer months. Whilst some are still imported, you cannot beat the sweet flavour of the home-grown produce. If you have the chance, get out to the countryside and pick your own, or make the most of the seasonal prices in the shops.

Berries are particularly low in calories, they are an excellent source of vitamin C and their versatility is endless - you can use them to make jams, jellies, pies, fruit tarts and sauces. They can even be used to produce liqueurs.

When buying, make sure that the fruit is not bruised, musty or mouldy. If you are lucky, you may be able to buy them loose. Otherwise they are sometimes sold in traditional punnets, although they are more likely to come in plastic containers nowadays. As soon as possible after buying, remove the fruit from the containers, discard any spoilt berries and place the remaining fruit loosely in a dish or tray until required.

Remember, buy only as many as you can eat at one time.

Baked Omelette with Marinated Berries

Serves 4

CALORIES
Approximately 365 per portion

INGREDIENTS: FILLING
9 oz/250 g mixed berries, e.g. strawberries, raspberries, blackberries, redcurrants
1 tbsp sugar
2 fl oz/50 ml orange liqueur
4 tbsp raspberry jam
icing sugar to finish

OMELETTE
5 egg whites
4 egg yolks
3 oz/75 g caster sugar
1 oz/25 g butter, melted
2 tsp single cream
½ tsp vanilla extract
1½ oz/40 g flour
¼ tsp lemon rind, grated
1 pinch cardamom powder and ginger
butter to grease the pan

OVEN TEMPERATURE
170°C/325°F/Gas Mark 3

METHOD:

FILLING
Mix all the berries with the orange liqueur and sugar and keep aside.

OMELETTE
Whisk the egg whites with a quarter of the sugar until stiff. Keep aside in the refrigerator.

Mix the egg yolks and remaining sugar in a bowl and whisk until creamy so that when you lift the whisk it forms a ribbon.

Add the melted butter, cream and vanilla and whisk for another 2 minutes.
Fold in the stiff egg white and the flour alternately.
Add the lemon rind, ginger and cardamom powder.
Heat the butter in an omelette pan, pour in the mixture and cook until firm.
Alternatively pour the mixture into a well greased baking tray roughly 1 in/2.5 cm deep and bake in the oven for about 20 minutes until the mixture is firm.

TO FINISH OFF
Drain the berries in a sieve and add the liquid to the raspberry jam. Heat and keep aside.

Remove the omelette from the pan and place on a serving dish. Place the berries on one half of the omelette. Then pour the warm jam mixture over and fold the omelette. Dust with icing sugar. Garnish with mint and serve.

Seasonal Berries with a Sherry Sauce

Serves 6

CALORIES
Approximately 255 per portion

INGREDIENTS:

BERRIES
1 tbsp sweet sherry
2 tbsp sugar
11 oz/300 g strawberries
11 oz/300 g raspberries
(or any other berries in season)

SHERRY CREAM
7 fl oz/200 ml whipping cream, cold
5 fl oz/150 ml sweet sherry
2 fl oz/50 ml white wine
4 egg yolks
5 tbsp sugar
1 tsp gelatine powder
4 egg whites, cold
½ tsp lemon rind

METHOD:

BERRIES

Mix the sherry with the sugar until it is dissolved.

Cut the strawberries in half. Place the strawberries and raspberries on a plate and pour the sherry and sugar liquid over them. Keep aside.

SHERRY CREAM

Whip the cream until stiff. Keep aside in the refrigerator. Use a whisk to mix the sherry, white wine, 3 tbsp sugar and egg yolks in a bowl set over a pan of simmering water. Whisk constantly until thick. Do not allow the water to boil.

Remove from the heat immediately and whisk for a further 3 minutes.

Sprinkle over the gelatine and whisk in. Pass through a sieve into a bowl. Add the lemon rind.

Place the bowl over a pan of cold water for about 10-15 minutes. Stir frequently until the mixture is cold and starting to set.

While the mixture is cooling, whisk the egg whites, gradually adding the remaining 2 tbsp sugar. Whisk until stiff. Place in the refrigerator until required. When the egg yolk mixture is cold, fold in the whipped cream and stiff egg white using a spatula.

TO FINISH OFF

Place the berries in glasses or bowls. Pour the cream mixture on top and refrigerate overnight.

Garnish with fresh berries and mint.

STIFF EGG WHITES

In many recipes I use stiffly beaten egg white. Although this sounds simple, there are times when the white just won't stiffen, no matter how long and hard you beat. To ensure that this doesn't happen, follow these tips:

- The egg white must be cold and completely free from any trace of egg yolk.
- The bowl and whisk must be perfectly clean and free from any grease.
- Start by whisking slowly and then gradually speed up.
- If you need to add sugar, add it spoonful by spoonful until the egg white is stiff, all the sugar is incorporated and no sugar granules are left.
- Always use straight away.

BRUSSELS SPROUTS

Like cabbage, the smaller Brussels sprout is a most under-rated vegetable. Too often overcooked to tastelessness, its reputation is slightly tarnished. Treated in the correct manner, however, the Brussels sprout will provide a sweet and nutty addition to any meal.

Available most of the year, sprouts are most popular in autumn and winter, as their flavour is improved by frost. Look for those which are about the size of a walnut and are firm and green. Avoid those which resemble small cabbages, particularly if they are yellowing and wilting - the flavour will be inferior.

Occasionally you may find red sprouts on sale or growing in your garden. Their flavour is good but unfortunately they will lose their rosy colour and turn green on cooking.

Once purchased, sprouts will keep well in the refrigerator for about 3 days. Usually they are boiled to cook, but try them baked, steamed or even sautéed. They may be served as a vegetable accompaniment, seasoned to taste with some chopped caraway seeds, or creamed, or with a white wine or cheese sauce. Another delicious alternative is to toss them in sour cream and nutmeg before serving, or use them as a salad.

Try my favourite: toss freshly steamed sprouts with fried tofu cubes and crisp bacon.

Never let it be said that the Brussels sprout is boring!

Cream of Brussels Sprout and Chestnut Soup

Serves 4

CALORIES
Approximately 190 per portion

INGREDIENTS
1 lb/450 g Brussels sprouts
1 oz/25 g butter or margarine
1 shallot or ¼ onion, peeled and finely chopped
½ clove garlic, peeled and crushed
2 oz/50 g chestnuts, coarsely chopped (frozen or tinned and drained), keep 2 tbsp for garnish
1¼ pt/750 ml vegetable stock
5 fl oz/150 ml single cream
salt & freshly ground white pepper

GARNISH
2 tbsp chestnuts, chopped (from above)
2 tbsp sliced Brussels sprout rings (from above)

METHOD
Remove the dark green leaves and cut the sprouts into fine rings. Cook 2 tbsp of the sprout rings in salted water until tender but still crisp. Refresh in cold water, drain and keep aside for garnish.

Melt the butter or margarine in a saucepan. Sweat the shallots or onion and the garlic until transparent but without colouring. Add the remaining sprout rings and sweat for 2 minutes.

Add the chestnuts and vegetable stock, cover with a lid and simmer gently for about 30 minutes.

Add the cream and boil (without a lid) for a further 5 minutes. Puree the soup and pass through a sieve into a saucepan. Bring to the boil. If necessary, add more stock to thin it down, and season.

TO FINISH OFF
Add the chopped chestnuts and reserved Brussels sprouts rings before serving. Toasted slices of French bread would be a good accompaniment to this soup.

Brussels Sprout and Bacon Flan

Serves 4

CALORIES
Approximately 425 per portion

INGREDIENTS:

PASTRY
4 oz/125 g wholemeal flour
2 oz/50 g margarine, room temperature
3 tbsp cold water
1 tsp sunflower oil
pinch of salt & freshly ground pepper

FILLING
5 oz/150 g fresh Brussels sprouts
5 oz/150 g leeks
1 tsp vegetable oil
4 rashers of bacon, cut into strips
1 shallot or ¼ onion, peeled and finely chopped
4 fl oz/100 ml white wine
2 eggs, size 3, beaten
4 fl oz/100 ml milk
1 tsp flour
2 oz/50 g Cheddar cheese, grated
salt & freshly ground white pepper
pinch grated nutmeg

GARNISH
a few bacon rashers (optional)

OVEN TEMPERATURE
200°C/400°F/Gas Mark 6

METHOD:

PASTRY
Mix together the salt and flour in a large bowl. Rub in the margarine until the mixture resembles fine breadcrumbs. Add the water and oil to the mixture and quickly knead to a soft dough.

Cover with clingfilm and rest in the refrigerator for 30 minutes.

FILLING
Remove the dark green leaves from the Brussels sprouts and cut the sprouts into rings. Keep aside.

Use the white part of the leek and cut into rings. Keep aside.

Heat the oil in a large non-stick pan. Add the bacon and fry until golden brown. Reduce the heat and add the shallot or onion. Sweat until transparent but without colouring.

Add the leek and Brussels sprout rings and sweat for 1 minute. Add the white wine, cover and simmer for about 2 minutes on a low heat. Season with salt and pepper. Remove from the heat and drain. Leave to cool.

Mix together the eggs, milk and flour in a large bowl, then add the cheese. Add the leek and Brussels sprout mixture and combine well.

TO FINISH OFF
Roll out the dough and use to line an 8 in/20 cm flan ring. Prick with a fork and bake in the oven for 5 minutes. Remove from the oven and rest for 25 minutes. Spoon in the filling and bake for a further 30 minutes until cooked. Remove from the oven and leave for 5 minutes to set before serving.

Grill or fry a few bacon rashers until crisp and use as garnish.

PREPARING BRUSSELS SPROUTS

Brussels sprouts need very little preparation. Simply trim the stalks and remove the outer green leaves. If the sprouts are large, cut a cross in their stems to aid cooking. Small sprouts do not need this, and, in fact, it will only spoil their shape.
NEVER OVERCOOK: **7 minutes in boiling salted water will be quite sufficient.**

LEEKS

These onion flavoured vegetables are available from October until May, making them a welcome winter vegetable. Their thick stems are composed of tightly packed slim thin layers, which branch at the top to dark green leaves. Their size can vary quite enormously.

When buying leeks, look for well-shaped straight vegetables, avoiding any that are yellowing, or have slimy leaves. Preferably choose small to medium-sized ones, as over-large leeks may be woody, particularly late in the season.

To use, remove the coarse outer leaves, trim the top and root ends and wash thoroughly to remove any sand or grit.

Cook in boiling salted water for 12-15 minutes, then add a little melted butter or a white sauce. Alternatively, slice thinly and stir-fry for about 5 minutes, until cooked but still crisp. Leeks are also delicious braised in a little stock in the oven, or in a soup during the cold winter months. For something more adventurous, try leek fried with mushrooms with a light soya sauce, leek and ham gratin or deep-fried Camembert with leek sauce.

The young, tender leeks found in the spring, finely shredded, make an interesting addition to a salad. They are also delicious blanched and tossed in a vinaigrette or mayonnaise dressing. Naturally, leeks are served not only as a vegetable, but also as an ingredient in many recipes.

Pancakes Filled with Leek and Tuna

Serves 4

CALORIES
Approximately 720 per portion

INGREDIENTS
vegetable oil to cook the pancakes
3 oz/75 g flour
5 fl oz/150 ml milk
2 eggs, lightly beaten
salt & freshly ground white pepper
½ tsp herbs (e.g. parsley, tarragon, dill), finely chopped

FILLING
1 tbsp vegetable oil
1 medium onion or 3 shallots, peeled and finely chopped
1 clove garlic, peeled and crushed
7 oz/200 g leek, dark green leaves removed, finely diced
4 fl oz/100 ml vegetable stock
10 oz/300 g tinned tuna, drained and flaked
2 tbsp mayonnaise
salt & freshly ground pepper

SAUCE
drained cooking liquid
8 fl oz/250 ml single cream
salt & freshly ground pepper

OVEN TEMPERATURE
180°C/350°F/Gas Mark 4

METHOD:

PANCAKES
Mix all the ingredients together and leave to rest for 30 minutes.

In the meantime, prepare the filling.

FILLING
Heat the vegetable oil. Add the onion, garlic and white of leek and sweat until transparent, but without colouring.

Add the vegetable stock, cover and simmer on a low heat for 4-5 minutes. Remove the lid. Add the tuna and heat.

Remove from the heat, add the mayonnaise and season to taste.

Place in a sieve and press gently to drain. Keep the liquid for the sauce. You will have about 2 tbsp.

SAUCE
Bring the above cooking liquid to the boil, together with the cream, and boil until a creamy consistency is obtained. Season and keep aside.

PANCAKES
Brush a non-stick pan with oil.

Add a thin layer of pancake mixture, reduce the heat and cook until golden brown on both sides.

Repeat until all the mixture is used up.

TO FINISH OFF
Spoon the filling equally onto each pancake. Roll up the pancakes and place next to each other in an oven-proof dish. Pour the sauce over and bake in the oven for 15-20 minutes.

Leek and Salmon Casserole with Sour Cream (left) & Pancakes Filled with Leek and Tuna (right)

Leek and Salmon Casserole with Sour Cream

Serves 4

CALORIES
Approximately 375 each

INGREDIENTS
2 tbsp vegetable oil
1 shallot or ¼ onion, peeled and finely chopped
½ clove garlic, peeled and crushed
11 oz/300 g leek, dark leaves removed, cut into rings
7 fl oz/200 ml white wine
1 pt/600 ml fish stock
1 large potato, peeled, cut in half lengthwise and cut into thick slices
2 tbsp sour cream
1 lb/450 g salmon fillet, no skin, cut into thumb-size cubes
¼ tsp dill
salt & freshly ground white pepper

METHOD

Heat the vegetable oil in a saucepan. Sweat the shallot or onion and the garlic until transparent, but without colouring.

Add the leek and sweat for a further minute. Add the white wine and fish stock and boil for 10 minutes. Add the potato, bring to the boil and simmer for 5-10 minutes until cooked.

Add the sour cream, bring to the boil and season. Add the dill and salmon cubes. Remove from the heat immediately, cover with a lid and leave for 5 minutes so that the cubes cook.

This can be served with slices of French bread topped with melted cheese.

CLEANING LEEKS

Leeks need to be thoroughly cleaned to remove all the grit caught in the leaves. To do this, split them to within 2 in/5 cm of the base, and flick back the leaves under running water to ensure that all particles are removed.

CHOCOLATE

For many of us chocolate is an irresistible passion! Products fall into several categories, and flavours vary from country to country, but the main ingredients are always the same. Cocoa mass ("raw" chocolate pressed from cacao nuts) and cocoa butter (the fat from the nuts) form the basic ingredients, together with varying quantities of sugar, milk solids and flavourings.

Whilst milk and white chocolate are most popular for eating, their mild flavour makes them less suitable for culinary purposes. Plain chocolate, on the other hand, is more often used for cooking, because of its rich flavour. Couverture is the chocolate form which is usually favoured by the professionals, because of its high proportion of cocoa butter and smooth texture - however it is expensive and difficult to use.

For home baking, plain chocolate is usually the best buy. So-called "cooking" chocolate, whilst more economical, has other fats added, such as coconut oil, which give it a less pure flavour.

Of course, cocoa powder is probably the most economical method of obtaining a rich chocolate flavour. For the best result, the powder must be mixed with a boiling liquid.

Chocolate Flans

Makes 6 flans

CALORIES
Approximately 345 calories per flan

INGREDIENTS
10 fl oz/300 ml milk
8 fl oz/250 ml single cream
vanilla essence
4 oz/125 g plain chocolate, coarsely chopped
1 tbsp rum
6 egg yolks
4 tbsp sugar

GARNISH
whipped cream

OVEN TEMPERATURE
170°C/335°F/Gas Mark 3

METHOD

Mix together the milk, cream, vanilla essence and chocolate pieces and heat until the chocolate melts.

Add the rum. Remove from the heat. Mix the egg yolks and sugar together thoroughly using a whisk. Still using a whisk, add the milk, cream and chocolate mixture to the sugar and egg yolk mixture (not the other way round, otherwise the eggs will curdle).

Pour the mixture into 6 ramekin dishes. Place a sheet of newspaper on the bottom of a roasting tray. Fill the pan with hot water. Place the ramekin dishes in the water in the pan, making sure that the water comes three-quarters of the way up the ramekins. Place in the oven and poach (do not boil) for about 45 minutes.

Remove the pan from the oven and leave the ramekin dishes to cool in the pan. Remove the ramekin dishes and leave in the refrigerator until cold. Before serving garnish with some whipped cream.

MELTING CHOCOLATE
Many recipes call for melted chocolate. This isn't difficult to do, but you have to know the rules if you don't want it to burn, go dull or develop a white haze. The secret of success is to keep the temperature as low as possible. You can use any one of three methods, but always start by breaking the chocolate into small pieces, as it will then take less time to melt. Microwaving is ideal: place the chocolate in a small microwave dish, cover and microwave on medium. Alternatively melt it in a bowl at 75°C in the oven or place over a pan of simmering water - never allowing moisture to come into contact with the chocolate.

Valentine's Cake

Makes about 12 slices

CALORIES
Approximately 380 calories per slice

INGREDIENTS
9 oz/250 g flour
3 tbsp cocoa
1 tsp bicarbonate of soda
9 oz/250 g sugar
½ tsp salt
5 tbsp oil
1 tbsp vinegar
1 tsp vanilla
8 oz/250 ml water
smooth apricot jam

CHOCOLATE GLAZE
3 tbsp butter
2 tbsp cocoa
5 oz/150 g icing sugar
1 egg white, unbeaten

GARNISH (OPTIONAL)
whipped cream and grated chocolate

OVEN TEMPERATURE
180°C/350°F/Gas Mark 4

METHOD
Mix together the flour, cocoa, bicarbonate of soda, sugar and salt. Make a well in the centre and pour in the oil, vinegar, vanilla and water.

Stir vigorously with a wooden spoon until blended. Pour into a loaf tin and bake for 50-60 minutes. Cool, then turn out.

When the cake is completely cold, cut it in half horizontally, spread with apricot jam and sandwich together.

GLAZE
Melt the butter and stir in the cocoa. Blend the sugar with the egg white. Add this to the butter and cocoa mixture and stir over a low heat until blended. Pour over the cake.
Garnish with whipped cream and chocolate if desired.

CHRISTMAS

Late December has long been established as a time of celebration. Early civilisations worshipped their gods in a frenzy of eating and drinking, and rather than banish the existing pagan customs, the early Christian church named December 25 as the birthday of Christ.

The Christmas period is a time of enthusiastic socialising, all too often making it hard work for the cook in the family, as relatives and friends drop by to exchange greetings and presents.

The following recipes provide some appropriate snacks and meals for a range of potential Christmas scenarios - from the pre-Christmas drinks parties to the all too familiar post-Christmas turkey left-overs blues!

Christmas cookies are very popular on the Continent at this time of year. They store well and make an ideal standby with a cup of tea or a mug of coffee when friends drop by. Alternatively, make all the cookies and wrap them in pretty boxes to give away as presents or use them as edible decorations for your tree.

Above all, Christmas time means party time. Parties are great fun, but they often involve a great deal of hard work for the host. Whatever the scale of your entertaining, the key to success lies in careful planning. Planning ahead will leave you more confident on the night, so that you can relax and enjoy yourself. After all the party is for you too! Offer a selection of appetising snacks, which can be prepared in advance. In addition to the two party snacks recipes below, try prunes wrapped in bacon and grilled, grissini sticks wrapped in slices of Parma ham or vol-au-vent cases filled with vegetable curry, minced meat or prawns.

Last but not least, the Christmas turkey! Turkeys range from about 6 lb (2.7 kg) to almost 40 lb (18 kg). The most popular size is about a 10 lb (4.5 kg) dressed bird, which will serve eight people. When deciding what size of turkey you need, allow about 12 oz (350 g) dressed weight per serving.

If you buy a frozen bird, it must be allowed to defrost naturally (if possible in the refrigerator) and thoroughly before cooking. This can take up to 48 hours. Once defrosted, try to use the bird on the same or following day. Turkey meat is not particularly strong in flavour and is greatly enhanced by the addition of a good stuffing or forcemeat. As an alternative to the traditional sausage meat and chestnut stuffings, try the more unusual combinations of ingredients in the recipes below.

All good things come to an end, however, and once the fun of Christmas is over, every year we are faced with the dilemma of what to do with the turkey that remains. Many a family cringes at the thought of endless turkey sandwiches! The recipes in this section include some new ideas for transforming your left-overs into delicious meals.

Spinach and Ricotta Cheese Turnovers

Makes about 30-35 turnovers

CALORIES
Approximately 90 calories per turnover

INGREDIENTS
10 oz/300 g spinach leaves (fresh or frozen)
1 tbsp vegetable oil
2 oz/50 g bacon
1 tbsp shallot or onion, chopped
1 tbsp Ricotta cheese, drained and cut into small cubes
salt & freshly ground white pepper
1 lb 5oz/600 g puff pastry
1 egg, beaten, for egg wash

OVEN TEMPERATURE
220° C/425° F/Gas Mark 7

METHOD
Cook the spinach leaves in salted water. Refresh in cold water, drain and press down well with your hands to extract any remaining water. Chop coarsely.
Heat the vegetable oil in a non-stick pan. Add the bacon and brown slightly.
Add the shallots or onion and sweat for about 1 minute without colouring. Add the spinach and cheese cubes. Season with salt and pepper.
Place in a sieve and leave to cool.
Roll out the puff pastry ⅛ in/2 mm thick. Using a cutter, cut out round shapes, 3 in/7 cm in diameter. (Freeze the pastry trimmings for future use).
Let the circles rest for 30 minutes.

TO FINISH OFF
Place some spinach and cheese filling in the centre of each circle.
Brush around the edges with the egg and then fold the pastry circles to make half moon shapes. Press together firmly with the back of the cutter.
Brush with egg wash and bake for about 12-15 minutes.

Party snacks

Stilton Balls with Walnuts and Sesame Seeds

Makes about 30 balls

CALORIES
Approximately 50 per ball

INGREDIENTS
5 oz/150 g Stilton cheese
1½ oz/40 g butter, at room temperature
1 tsp chopped shallot or onion
1 tsp parsley, finely chopped
1 tsp Port wine
2 tbsp crème fraiche or cream cheese
salt & freshly ground white pepper
3 oz/75 g walnuts, coarsely chopped
1 tbsp sesame seeds, roasted under the grill until golden brown

METHOD
With a whisk or hand blender, mix together the Stilton and butter. Add the shallots or onion and the parsley. Add the Port wine and crème fraiche (or cream cheese) and mix. Season. Leave in the refrigerator for about 2 hours until the mixture is stiff.

Using a spoon, divide the mixture into pieces the size of a walnut. Wet your hands and form the pieces into ball shapes. Keep aside.

TO FINISH OFF
Mix together the chopped walnuts and sesame seeds. Roll the cheese balls in this mixture, arrange on a plate and serve.

QUANTITIES FOR SNACKS

For a 1½ hour drinks party, prepare about 6 types of snacks. For a 3 hour party, about 9 - some of which should be more substantial, as some guests may make them their meal. Allow one or two of each type of snack per guest.

Guests generally prefer something hot, but remember that the more hot food you plan, the more time you'll need in the kitchen - so be realistic and limit it to 2 or 3.

Basic Cookie Dough

Makes about 60 cookies

CALORIES
Approximately 90 per cookie

INGREDIENTS
9 oz/250 g unsalted butter, cold and cut into small cubes
5 oz/150 g icing sugar
4 egg yolks
few drops vanilla and lemon essence
14 oz/400 g soft plain flour
5 oz/150 g ground almonds

OVEN TEMPERATURE
180°C/350°F/Gas Mark 4

METHOD
Mix together the cold butter and icing sugar. Add the egg yolks and the vanilla and lemon essence. Mix in the flour and ground almonds.

Knead quickly to a dough, being careful not to over-knead. Wrap in clingfilm and leave in the refrigerator for about 1 hour. Remove from the refrigerator, cut into three equal portions and use to make Vanilla Crescents, Triestini and Iced Stars as described below. Keep the dough in the refrigerator prior to use.

STORING COOKIES

The best way to store your cookies is to wrap them in a plastic bag which can be sealed, or, even better, store the cookies in an airtight tin and they will keep very well for a few weeks. The dough can also be frozen, raw or cooked.

Vanilla Crescents

Use Basic Cookie Dough as above

ADDITIONAL INGREDIENTS
caster sugar for coating
icing sugar for dusting

OVEN TEMPERATURE
180°C/350°F/Gas Mark 4

METHOD
Roll out the dough into a sausage shape about 1¼ in/3 cm diameter. Cut into slices about ½ in/1 cm thick.

Roll each slice by hand into a small cigar shape (ie. a little thicker in the middle). Roll in caster sugar. Form into half moon shapes.

Bake in the oven for about 12-15 minutes. Dust with icing sugar.

Triestini

Use Basic Cookie Dough as above

ADDITIONAL INGREDIENTS
3 oz/75 g flaked almonds, slightly crushed
1 egg and 2 tbsp milk mixed together to make an egg wash
15 glacé cherries, cut in half, or red jam

OVEN TEMPERATURE
180° C/350° F/Gas Mark 4

METHOD
Roll out the dough to ¼ in/5 mm thick. Using a cutter, cut out round shapes about 2 in/5 cm in diameter. Brush one side with egg wash and cover with flaked almonds. Put half a cherry or a small blob of red jam in the centre. Bake for 12-15 minutes.

Iced Stars

Use Basic Cookie Dough as above

ADDITIONAL INGREDIENTS
juice of half a lemon mixed together with 4 heaped tbsp icing sugar to form a fairly stiff mixture

egg wash from above

OVEN TEMPERATURE
180°C/350°F/Gas Mark 4

METHOD
Roll out the dough to about ¼ in/5 mm thick. Using a cutter, cut out star shapes. Brush half the quantity with egg wash. Bake in the oven for about 10-12 minutes. When cold, brush those which weren't brushed with egg wash with the lemon and icing sugar mixture.

Rice Stuffing with Dried Apricots and Curry Powder

INGREDIENTS

(to stuff a bird up to 14 lb/6.3 kg)

2 tbsp vegetable oil

2 oz/50 g onion or shallot, peeled and finely chopped

7 oz/200 g long grain rice

1 tsp curry powder

4 fl oz/100 ml white wine

2 oz/50 g dried apricots, diced

2 oz/50 g sultanas

¼ stick cinnamon

pinch aniseed powder

18 fl oz/500 ml chicken stock

salt & freshly ground pepper

OVEN TEMPERATURE

160°C /325°F/Gas Mark 3

METHOD

Heat the oil in a saucepan. Add the onion or shallot and sweat until transparent but without colouring.

Add the rice and sweat for a few seconds. Add the curry powder then the white wine and bring to the boil. Add the apricots, sultanas, cinnamon and aniseed. Add the chicken stock and bring to the boil.

Cover with a lid and cook in the oven for 15 minutes. Remove from the oven, season and leave to cool.

Use to stuff the turkey.

Pistachio and Pine Kernel Stuffing

INGREDIENTS
(to stuff a bird up to 14 lb/6.3 kg)
2 tbsp vegetable oil
1 onion, peeled and chopped
7 oz/200 g pistachio nuts, coarsely chopped
7 oz/200 g pine kernels, coarsely chopped
5 oz/150 g pork sausage meat
2 tsp sage, chopped
4 tsp breadcrumbs
salt & freshly ground pepper

METHOD
Heat the vegetable oil in a saucepan. Add the onion and sweat until transparent, but without colouring. Add the pistachio nuts and pine kernels and leave to cool.

Mix with the sausage meat. Add the sage and breadcrumbs, and season.

Use to stuff the turkey.

Turkey Lasagne with Chillis

Serves 6

CALORIES
Approximately 570 calories per portion

INGREDIENTS
12 green lasagne sheets (buy lasagne which is labelled "no pre-cook, ready to use")
2 tbsp vegetable oil
1 shallot or ¼ onion, peeled and finely chopped
½ clove garlic, peeled and crushed
17½ oz/500 g cold, cooked turkey, cut into strips or cubes

TOMATO SAUCE
2 tbsp vegetable oil
½ onion, peeled and finely chopped
½ clove garlic, crushed
½ small red chilli, seeds removed and finely chopped
6 medium tomatoes, peeled and coarsely chopped (or tinned tomatoes, drained)
4 fl oz/100 ml chicken or turkey stock

CHEESE SAUCE
1½ oz/40 g butter
2 oz/50 g flour
1 pt/600 ml chicken, turkey or vegetable stock
3 fl oz/75 ml milk
salt & freshly ground pepper
2 oz/50 g Cheddar cheese

OVEN TEMPERATURE
200°C/400°F/Gas Mark 6

METHOD
Heat the vegetable oil in a non-stick pan. Add shallots or onion and the garlic and sweat until transparent but without colouring. Add the turkey pieces and sweat for a further 1-2 minutes. Remove and keep aside.

TOMATO SAUCE
Heat the vegetable oil. Sweat the onion and garlic until transparent, but without colouring. Add the chilli. Add the tomatoes and stock and cook on a medium heat for about 10 minutes. Season and keep aside.

CHEESE SAUCE
Heat the butter gently, add the flour and stir on a low heat for half a minute. Add half of the cold stock and bring to the boil, stirring constantly. Add the remaining stock and the milk and simmer for about 20 minutes. Add half the cheese and season with salt and pepper. Remove from the heat and keep aside.

TO FINISH OFF
Mix the turkey mixture with ¾ of the cheese sauce and season to taste. Keep the remainder of the cheese sauce to garnish the top layer of the lasagne. Cover the base of a medium sized, rectangular, oven-proof dish with a thin layer of chilli tomato sauce. Cover with a layer of lasagne sheets. Add a layer of the turkey mixture followed by a layer of lasagne sheets. Continue with the layers until all the ingredients are used up, but make sure that the last layer is lasagne. Pour over the remaining cheese sauce. Sprinkle over the remaining cheese and bake in the oven for about 25-30 minutes until cooked and golden brown.

Festive Salad

Serves 2

CALORIES

Approximately 650 calories per portion

INGREDIENTS

2 oz/50 g hard cheese
5 oz/150 g cooked ham, fat removed or cooked turkey
1 banana, ripe but firm
2 oz/50 g leaf salad of your choice

SAUCE

3 tbsp sherry or white wine vinegar
½ tsp mild mustard
1 shallot or onion, peeled and finely chopped
6 tbsp olive oil
salt & freshly ground white pepper
1 tsp chives, chopped
herbs to garnish

METHOD

Cut the ham or turkey and the cheese into cubes or strips and keep aside.

SAUCE

Mix together the vinegar, mustard and shallot or onion. Add the olive oil. Season with salt and freshly ground pepper. Add the chives.

TO FINISH OFF

Peel the banana, cut into slices and mix with the dressing immediately to prevent the banana from turning brown. Then mix in the ham or turkey and the cheese. Marinate for 5 minutes.

Wash the salad leaves, cut to a suitable size and arrange on a plate. Place the ham/turkey and cheese mixture in the centre. Garnish with herbs of your choice.

Turkey Steaks

Serves 2

CALORIES

Approximately 720 per portion

INGREDIENTS

3 tbsp vegetable oil
2 turkey steaks (each about 6 oz/175 g)

MARINADE

salt & freshly ground white pepper
pinch ground ginger
2 tsp light soya sauce
4 tsp dry sherry
pinch English mustard

SAUCE

1 oz/25 g butter
2 oz/50 g button mushrooms, sliced
7 fl oz/200 ml single cream
½ tsp lemon zest
1 egg yolk, lightly beaten

METHOD

Mix together all the ingredients for the marinade. Pour over the turkey steaks and marinate for about 30 minutes.

Drain and reserve the marinade for the sauce. Heat the oil in a non-stick pan and fry the turkey steaks until they are brown on both sides (they should still be pink inside). Place in an ovenproof dish and keep warm.

SAUCE

Heat the butter in a saucepan, add the mushrooms and brown slightly.
Add the marinade and bring to the boil.
Add the cream and boil until a creamy consistency is obtained.
Add lemon zest and season with salt and freshly ground pepper. Leave to cool.
Add the egg yolk. Pour the sauce over the turkey steaks and brown under the grill.

DELICIOUS TURKEY

The secrets to a delicious turkey are as follows:

* Fill both cavities with a flavourful stuffing to enhance the flavour of your bird.
* Rub the bird generously with butter, cover with streaky bacon and wrap in foil. This will prevent the breast from getting too dry. Remove the foil and bacon 45 minutes before the end of cooking time.
* Cook slowly at 160°C/325°F/Gas Mark 3, allowing 20 minutes per 1 lb/450 g plus an additional 20 minutes.
* Before serving, test by piercing the thickest part of the thigh - the juices must be clear.

INDEX